The Kundalini Process

A Christian Perspective

by

Philip St. Romain

Published by Contemplative Ministries, Inc.
Bel Aire, KS

2017

Printed by Lulu Press

ISBN: 978-1-387-29582-1

See http://shalomplace.com/psrbks.html for other format options.

Purple swirl image on front cover from http://canitbesaturdaynow.com/

Scripture quotes from New International Version of the Bible unless otherwise noted

Contents

Tables and Figures

Tables

Figures

Note to Publishers

This work is self-published, but can easily be un-published.

Publishers who are interested in contracting for print and/or digital rights can contact me through the online Contact form at philstromain.com.

Philip St. Romain
October 2017

Introduction

In 1985, I began to experience an array of confusing phenomena that seemed to be related to a deepening of my prayer life. There were inner lights (beautiful swirling blue and gold tones) sensations of energy pushing up into my brain, spontaneous bodily movements similar to yogic positions, and many other unusual symptoms. In corresponding with friends and spiritual directors, I was introduced to the literature on kundalini energy, and this seemed to provide a satisfactory explanation to account for my experiences. Eventually, I wrote a book to describe them and to reflect on the psychological, physiological, spiritual, and theological implications of this process.[1] Fr. Thomas Keating, O.C.S.O., wrote the Introduction, a kindness I shall never forget.

A lot has happened since 1985. The book didn't stay in print very long, as sales were poor. Christians were unfamiliar with kundalini, and those non-Christians who knew about it seemed suspicious of a "Christian" treatment of this topic. But it did break the ice concerning a topic that had not yet received much attention in the Christian community. I also became identified as someone with whom people felt they could discuss unusual experiences they'd had or were having, some of which seemingly had nothing to do with kundalini. For example, I received a phone call from a woman who had a problem levitating at random times. She wanted to know what to do about this. Then there was the visit from a different woman who claimed she experienced bi-location, spending many nights helping frightened Chinese children who were living in caves. There were dozens of letters as well, and once the Internet

---

[1] *Kundalini Energy and Christian Spirituality: A Pathway to Growth and Healing* (New York, NY: Crossroads Publ., 1991).

7

became established, even more communication. I set up a web site — shalomplace.com — with a discussion forum on kundalini and spiritual emergency issues. To date, I have received emails from over 900 people, and the discussion forum has developed into a wonderful, supportive community, where people could share stories and help one another. There are close to 250 open discussions, with hundreds of posts and hundreds of thousands of views.

I have learned a great deal about spiritual transformation from these encounters and discussions, and yet I still do not consider myself an expert on this topic. What I am, professionally, is a Christian spiritual director, and I am quick to refer those in kundalini distress to meet with a kundalini counselor (there are a few that I've come to trust). But there's no doubt that part of the healing and integration for many comes from understanding what they're going through. These "kundalini Christians," as some have called themselves, need to know that they're not under demonic influence, as some of their pastors have told them, and that they are still "on the map" in their journey to deepening union with God. Some have experimented with Eastern meditation disciplines and feel they're being somehow punished for doing so; others were involved in respected Christian involvements like Charismatic Renewal or centering prayer. Once they received basic orientation about the process and its purpose, it seemed that this understanding in itself helped them settle down.

About This Book

I have often been asked if I had plans to write a follow-up to *Kundalini Energy and Christian Spirituality,* and my response has always been no. I did eventually re-publish it in 2004 and 2010, adding two new appendixes and including an update on my own personal process. I had other writings that were more of a priority, and, besides, I was already very involved in the discussions at shalomplace.com. But I think the time has come to pull together learnings through the years, and that is what this work will attempt to do. It will not be a continuation of the first book, however: no part 2, or "the rest of the story," but a companion work, reflecting more deeply on the philosophical, spiritual and theological meaning of kundalini.

Kundalini is a universal phenomenon, found in every world religion and even outside the province of formal religious affiliation. It is more explicitly recognized in Eastern traditions like Hinduism, Buddhism and Taoism, but once one knows what to look for, signs of it can be recognized elsewhere. Furthermore, human nature is human nature, no matter what religion one belongs to, so ultimately we can expect a great deal of convergence among the world religions at the level of anthropology, and this will help us to compare teachings about kundalini found among different traditions. Where we find significant differences beyond issues of semantics, there are possibilities for enhanced understandings.

I am entitling this work, *The Kundalini Process: A Christian Perspective,* as I think the approach I will take can help Christians better understand this phenomenon and its place in the spiritual life. I'm also hopeful that it will help non-Christians knowledgeable of kundalini come to a deeper appreciation of Christian theology and philosophy. My hope is that the end product will be the book I most needed when I began to search for guidance and understanding of the puzzling experiences I began to have over 30 years ago — a work that is straightforward, readable, practical, pastoral, compatible with Christian theology and spirituality, and faithful to the spirit of how kundalini is understood and worked with in the East. That's a tall order, I realize, and it will no doubt be somewhat deficient in one or more of these objectives. But I've had many years of dialogue with wonderful people to delve into all of these areas.

Acknowledgements

First and foremost, I wish to thank my dear friends, Jim and Tyra Arraj, who were important dialogue partners with me during those early days of kundalini activation. Jim has since passed away, but an essay he published on a "Christian Philosophical Explanation of Kundalini Energy" will be foundational to this work. Look for it in Chapter 2, where it will be reprinted in its entirety.

The community that developed around discussions on kundalini at the Shalom Place Discussion Board[2] are also deserve special mention. There are too many individuals to single out by name, but they have shared experiences and engaged in respectful dialogue for almost two decades now. Many of them are Christians, but a good number are not. This has made for some beneficial exchanges.

A few of my spiritual directees have shared deeply of their kundalini struggles, and I have learned from them as well. Additionally, numerous email dialogue partners who are not directees have brought helpful understanding.

Authors whose writings have significantly influenced this work include Michael Washburn, Thomas Keating, Gopi Krishna, Lee Sannella, Daniel Helminiak, and Carla Mae Streeter, to name a few. You can find out more about them and others in the References section in the back.

---

[2] See http://shalomplace.org/eve/forums

Several people were given the first draft of this work for proofing and suggestions. Derek Cameron, Mateusz Stróżyński, Melissa Schultz and Jerry Truex replied with helpful feedback.

The ministry team at Heartland Center for Spirituality has always been supportive of my writing projects, and this work is no exception. So has my dear wife of over 40 years now, Lisa, who wrote an affirming Postscript to my earlier work on this topic.

1.

The Kundalini Process

(This chapter is being published free of charge, and presents a general overview of themes that will be discussed more deeply in the rest of the book. See http://shalomplace.com/psrbks.html for more info on purchase options and related books.)

Kundalini is a Sanskrit term meaning "coiled."[3] In ancient Indian spirituality, it came to refer to a powerful force that was dormant at the base of the spine, but which could, through careful disciplines, be intensified and directed through the central channel of the spinal cord to the brain, stimulating spiritual energy centers called chakras along the way. This process was fraught with dangers, as one could be seriously hurt if the movement of this energy went awry, so the mentorship of a spiritual adept who had successfully awakened and integrated this energy was strongly advised. In fact, this phenomena and the yogic practices that helped awaken and release it were considered "occult," which means "hidden." If all went well, the awakening produced in the recipient a sense of well-being, bliss, enlightenment, and often psychic gifts as well.

Indian teaching affirmed this as a sacred process. The energy at the base of the spine was Shakti, or divine energy, conceived as feminine — a goddess. In rising up the spine to the to brain and beyond, through the top of the head, Shakti attains union with Shiva, divine consciousness, usually imaged as male. The human being serving as a conduit for this sacred marriage is thus considered exceedingly fortunate, blessed, and participating in

---

[3] From *kundala,* ring.

divinity. Often, he or she is given an honorary title like yogi or guru, and is sought out for instruction and mentoring.

Segue to sometime around 2005, when I was traveling somewhere by plane and decided to duck into an airport bookstore in search of reading material. There, to my surprise, were several books in the self-help section on activating your chakras, or gently awakening the kundalini power for health and vitality. Having written my own book on this topic years before, and being conversant with the literature, I decided to skim through them and even bought one. It soon became clear that we were a long ways from the careful treatment of this topic evidenced in ancient India, and in many serious books on the topic I'd read while doing research for my own. We were entering a new phase, when kundalini yoga workshops and retreats began to appear more and more in the West, with attendees hoping to become more initiated into this process. I now even find web sites that provide a step-by-step process to awaken kundalini!

We have also entered a time in which the very term, *kundalini*, has come to take on new meaning. I myself was ambivalent about using it to describe my experiences, as I had not submitted myself to the kinds of practices described in the yogic literature, and had not experienced some of the phenomena described. A friend who was a Taoist adept and serious student of yoga assured me that what I was going through was kundalini, as did others who knew something about it. So I went along with their thinking, and I'm not sorry I did. Books on this topic that continued to be published, and people I came into dialogue with also favored an expanded understanding.

What is Kundalini?

It's not uncommon for words to undergo an evolution of meaning. All you have to do is check a dictionary for the definition of a word, and you'll often find several enumerated meanings, and significant variance from the original root word. I'm thinking something like this has happened with regard to "kundalini." The classical Hindu idea should be listed as definition #1, but a broader understanding can be included as #2 and maybe even #3 and more. These more recent definitions should not be in disagreement with #1, but would broaden it to include other kinds of disciplines and experiences of transformative energy processes.

Here's how an updated definition might go:

1. *The yogic life force that is held to lie coiled at the base of the spine until it is aroused and sent to the head to trigger enlightenment.*[4]

   - I will restrict the terms *kundalini rising* and *kundalini awakening* to this definition, as does much of the literature, and will not be referencing it very often, as I do not want to presume to be a spokesman for the yogic tradition.

2. *A spiritual transformation process entailing intensified flows of energy throughout the body, leading to healing and higher spiritual consciousness.*

   - I am calling this *kundalini activation.* It is not in contradiction to #1, but is broader, encompassing Taoist, Buddhist and even Hindu experiences of transformative energy processes. Additionally, it opens the possibility for people from other religions and even those who are not particularly religious to find their experiences described and

---

[4] From Merriam-Webster Dictionary online: https://www.merriam-webster.com/

validated in terms of kundalini process. In my use of definition #2, I will not be capitalizing kundalini, for I am not meaning to refer to Shakti or any other aspect of Hindu mythology and theology.

I am also inclined to a third definition, as follows:

3. *The inner dynamism at work in human development, in general, "pushing" us from within to deepening spiritual growth and integration.*[5]
    - Michael Washburn's idea of the Dynamic Ground of consciousness accommodates this understanding.[6] For Washburn, this inner Ground is our deepest source of energy and the ultimate animator of our growth and embodiment. He equates this influence with kundalini and provides a comprehensive account of our developmental unfolding in terms of the Ego's relationship with the inner Ground. The idea here is that kundalini is at work in everyone — even those who do not evidence the dramatic energy phenomena — but at a lower level of intensity. Its evolutionary impetus is the same, only its unfolding is usually slow and gradual.[7] I am calling this the *kundalini dynamic.* In this sense, kundalini is similar to Jung's writings on individuation, which differs in its focus on wholeness and integrating opposing tendencies in the psyche.

---

[5] This is implied in the idea of the energy as "coiled" at the base of the spine, suggesting something like a spring that exerts a subtle tension.

[6] Michael Washburn, *The Ego and the Dynamic Ground: A Transpersonal Theory of Human Development* (Albany, NY: State University of New York Press, 1988).

[7] E.g., Joseph Chilton Pearce speaks of kundalini intensification during adolescence in *From Magical Child to Magical Teen* (Rochester, VT: Park Street Press, 2003).

I will use the term *kundalini process* or simply *kundalini* to refer to all of the above, as when I am referring to kundalini in general.

Some might wonder why propose definitions #2 and #3 rather than just use another term? My response is first, as noted above, I don't think the three definitions are in conflict; quite the contrary. The variation from 1 to 3 is by intensity more so than by kind — sort of like a volcano that is smoldering versus one in various stages of eruption. Second, because no matter what other term we might propose, people would reference it to kundalini. Remember that airport book? When a book on kundalini shows up in an airport bookstore, the term has become mainstream and has already broken free from its narrower origin.

Nevertheless, definition #2, in particular, does have a restricted focus, as there are many kinds of energy experiences that do not meet even this general definition. What makes kundalini unique is that this process, once activated, conduces toward *higher spiritual consciousness*, and not all energy experiences have this orientation. Many people have a variety of energy sensations in their bodies, sometimes painfully so. These can be caused by "pinched nerves," drugs, allergies, ascetical disciplines, etc. Not every energy sensation accompanying a spiritual discipline signifies kundalini activation. Many such are "arousals" — phenomena that die down after a short time. These might come during times of conversion or consolation, and be significant to the recipient. But kundalini process — especially awakening and activation — is ongoing and permanent. One can never go back to the way things were before.

Higher Spiritual Consciousness[8]

In noting that kundalini is oriented toward higher spiritual consciousness, we need to clarify what this term means and how it will be used in this book. The short response is that it means the kind of consciousness one experiences when the energy process aligns the powers of the soul called chakras with the innermost Ground of our being. We will discuss the meaning of these terms as we go along, but for now we note a few general characteristics of this experience:

a. Non-reflecting presence. Ability to just *be* with oneself, others, God, creation.

b. Intuitive understanding. Direct grasp of connections, meaning.

c. Deep sense of peace and contentment.

d. Feeling of being simply oneself without needing to define oneself.

e. Emotional equanimity; even-keeled.

f. Non-dual awareness; sense of connectedness with the creation.

g. Openness to transcendence, mystery.

h. Ability to take responsibility for thoughts.

These characteristics become increasingly established and integrated as the kundalini process advances.

Almost everyone experiences higher spiritual consciousness at some time, and we can even train ourselves through spiritual and psychological disciplines to explore this potentiality. This

---

[8] I am choosing to use this phrase rather than "enlightenment" in this book as Eastern understandings of the latter often differ somewhat from what I'm referring to.

brings up the point that some people evidence this consciousness but do not seem to have undergone kundalini activation. One explanation is that the process might be so low-key as to be imperceptible — the kundalini dynamic — or perhaps these people were already so well integrated that when the process intensified, they didn't encounter painful inner blockages to energy flow. I do not know. What is abundantly clear, however, is that the activated kundalini is all about "re-wiring" and cleansing the entire human system so that higher spiritual consciousness can become embodied, integrated and readily accessible. This takes time, which is why we speak of kundalini "process."

This brings up another point about which there is often much misunderstanding — namely that people who experience higher spiritual consciousness are not "stuck" there. They can still engage a situation rationally and reflectively, experience feelings, enjoy food and sex, make mistakes, and even sin. You might not even know you're interacting with a person who is in that state as they can seem very ordinary and normal. What is new is that the potentialities we had actualized earlier in life become ordered in the context of higher spiritual consciousness. Reflectivity happens in the context of non-reflectivity; walking and eating and sex in the context of a new capacity to be present to the moment; reading and relating with a new empathy. Not everything is compatible with this consciousness, however. One might discover that certain foods or books or tv shows disturb it, so one stays away from those. Finding a lifestyle compatible with this consciousness is a challenge, as excessive "noise" is most disruptive and distasteful.

Higher spiritual consciousness is not divine consciousness; it is still very much on the human side of reality. It often does happen that this development and union with God are concomitant, but not necessarily so. Ideally, the two journeys unfold together, with higher spiritual consciousness enabling deepening union with God, and deepening union with God providing the spiritual context for the inner healing and surrender that opens higher spiritual consciousness. We see the synchrony of these journeys in the great Saints and mystics of the religions of the world, who are models to us of what a beautiful human being is like. But even here, we need to carefully note that some Saints do not evidence higher spiritual consciousness. Most mystics and contemplative do, however. This is one reason why kundalini activation usually happens in the context of intense spiritual practice, and is very rare outside of this context.

Gopi Krishna liked to talk about kundalini as an evolutionary energy.[9] This brief treatment of higher spiritual consciousness could be one way of understanding what he was talking about: the awakening of potentialities in human nature that go well beyond the limitations of conventional, cultural Egoic consciousness.

Symptoms of Kundalini Activation

No two people have the same kundalini experience; each person's process is unique. Some have a very rough time of it while others find it smooth-sailing and enjoyable. It all depends on how much emotional healing is needed, the intensity of spiritual practice, the degree of stress in one's life, and many other factors. Age also seems to play a role. It's rare to find activation happening in people under 25 or over 60.

---

[9] See Gopi Krishna, *Kundalini: The Evolutionary Energy in Man* (Boston, MA: Shambhala, 1985). Also, Gene Kieffer's *Kundalini for the New Age: Selected Writings of Gopi Krishna* (Bantam, 1988).

Nevertheless, there is an array of symptoms that most people will evidence at some time or another during the process. It usually begins with a distinct sense that something has changed, or shifted within oneself. This can be very subtle — barely perceptible — or it can be quite explosive, with all sorts of inner fireworks going off. Generally, there is a peace about this shift, even though it might be accompanied by unsettling emotions or confusing energy phenomena. A sense of expanded consciousness emerges, sometimes very quickly. There is often a sense of inner guidance early on as well, especially in those who have a regular practice of prayer or meditation. "It's OK; this will be good for you" is the message that comes across, though not necessarily as a locution or anything like that. It's just a knowing. Sometimes there are guiding dreams as well.

The activation process can take a few weeks or months before it stabilizes. After that, things generally settle down, but one will always be aware of inner energy flow and occasional blockages, and one will have to adjust one's lifestyle to accommodate this new situation. While the early stages of the process unfold, one or more of the following symptoms might occur:[10]

- Involuntary jerks, tremors, shaking, itching, tingling, and crawling sensations, especially in the arms and legs [11]

- Energy rushes or feelings of electricity circulating the body

- Intense heat (sweating) or cold, especially as energy is experienced passing through the chakras

---

[10] This compilation from the Wikipedia entry on "Kundalini" is fairly representative of most lists. Chapter 6 on Kundalini Activation expands on this list in terms of kundalini's influence on the different levels of our human nature.

[11] I should add "ears" to this listing as well.

- Spontaneous pranayama, asanas, mudras and bandhas [12]
- Visions or sounds at times associated with a particular chakra
- Diminished or conversely extreme sexual desire sometimes leading to a state of constant or whole-body orgasm
- Emotional upheavals or surfacing of unwanted and repressed feelings or thoughts with certain repressed emotions becoming dominant in the conscious mind for short or long periods of time.
- Headache, migraine, or pressure inside the skull
- Increased blood pressure and irregular heartbeat
- Emotional numbness
- Antisocial tendencies
- Mood swings with periods of depression or mania
- Pains in different areas of the body, especially back and neck
- Sensitivity to light, sound, and touch
- Trance-like and altered states of consciousness
- Disrupted sleep pattern (periods of insomnia or oversleeping)
- Loss of appetite or overeating
- Bliss, feelings of infinite love and universal connectivity, transcendent awareness

Thankfully, these do not all happen at once, and some people only experience a few of them. Most with activated kundalini can continue to carry on with their everyday duties, though they will often be aware of strange sensations throughout the day.

---

[12] *Pranayama* is breathing patterns, *asanas* are body postures like those in yoga, *mudras* are hand gestures, *bandhas* are ways of locking parts of your body.

Disciplines for Activating Kundalini

After reading about the wonderful characteristics of higher spiritual consciousness and its connection with kundalini, many are often eager to have this experience themselves. I have been asked numerous times through the years if I would show people how to awaken this process, and I have always declined. My suggestion is to work on developing a relationship with God, and growing in that relationship, allowing the energy process to awaken on its own when the time is right. Dealing with the discomfiting symptoms described above is much easier if one has already developed a spiritual practice, as this can help to provide a "container" to hold and direct the energy.

Most of the people I've been in contact with had the energy process awaken as a consequence of contemplative disciplines. These include such practices as centering prayer, vipassana, TM, Zen and other meditative methods that move one to trans-conceptual consciousness. If one is also engaged in active practices to deepen virtue and facilitate healing, the mind will become increasingly still through the months and years. This changes the energy dynamics in the body/mind to accommodate the new consciousness that is emerging. Sometimes this is a gradual process, but with others, it can seem as though a "switch" of some kind is tripped at some point, opening new channels and patterns of energy flow within. *Energy follows attention.* That is a point we shall return to later in this book.

Shaktipat, a special energy touch, is another way to awaken kundalini. Years ago, I purchased *Kundalini Yoga for the West,*[13] by Swami Sivananda Radha, hoping to find deeper understanding and guidance for my own situation. Rather than

---

[13] Swami Sivananda Raddha, *Kundalini Yoga for the West* (Boston, MA: Shambhala, 1981)

saying much about kundalini, Swami Radha used the chakra system to present basic spiritual disciplines appropriate for each level. In a formal yoga practice such as she leads, the yogi keeps a discerning eye out for this readiness in the seeker. When the time is right, the teacher leads the seeker in a special ritual, and imparts shaktipat to quicken the energy in the student. This might consist of laying on of hands, a touch to the forehead, a short slap on the side of the face, or even a non-physical touch using the mind. But the point is, that shaktipat is usually administered with discretion, and only to those who are ready for the changes in energy dynamics it ignites.

That's the formal, responsible way to do things. Recently, however, I received an email from a young man who had just returned from pilgrimage in India, promising to communicate shaktipat to those who would join him for a special webinar (a pricey registration fee, of course). I don't know how much good that could do, but it would certainly be an example of non-physical shaktipat if it did work. *Siddha yoga* also makes use of shaktipat to activate the energy process, with a guru sometimes administering it to hundreds of people in a room at once.

There are also examples of people having kundalini awakened without practicing spiritual disciplines of any kind. One man reported recently that it happened to him as a consequence of studying philosophy. A young woman shared that she was just lying on her bed one day and started thinking about God, then light burst into the room and the process was awakened. Then there is the Charismatic Renewal (pentecostalism) in Christianity, where people lay on hands for baptism in the Spirit. Speaking in tongues and a wide range of psycho-somatic phenomena can accompany this experience. Joining up with such a prayer group while also practicing contemplative disciplines would be a good way for a Christian to prepare for kundalini activation. Spiritual direction is also advised.

Every religious culture with a mystical tradition knows of this process and treats it with great respect — even reverence. That's the best approach.

Coping with Kundalini

Kundalini process brings to light depths of woundedness that we were previously unaware of, and that can be most unpleasant. It is advisable to see a doctor or counselor if any of these symptoms become too intense or disturbing. Tell these professionals about kundalini if they don't seem to know about it, and encourage them to research the topic to find out more. If it should turn out that you need medication, don't worry about it. Take care of yourself. If you can eventually get off of the medication, that would be best, but be careful about this, and never do so without professional supervision.

What follows are a few practical suggestions for coping with discomfiting kundalini symptoms.[14]

1. Don't panic! Fear only colors the energy darkly. There is nothing to fear if you cooperate with the process (or at least don't frustrate it too much).

2. Find someone to talk to about what is happening to you — preferably someone who knows about kundalini or spiritual growth.

3. Accept the process as a sign of growth. Be grateful for the growth that is taking place within, painful though it may be.

---

[14] From Chapter 6 in *Kundalini Energy and Christian Spirituality: A Pathway to Growth and Healing,* by Philip St. Romain (New York, NY: Crossroads Publ., 1991).

4. Do not work against the process. Pay attention to what hurts, and back off on activities that seem to frustrate the process (e.g., heavy reading, drinking alcohol, using drugs, smoking, immoderate sex, even too much meditation). Learn to "go with the flow."

5. Keep your intent of consciousness focused on *being here now in love*.

6. Let the various states of consciousness produced by kundalini come and go. Experience and explore them, but do not attach to them. The True Self is not to be found in any particular state of consciousness.

7. Surrender yourself into the care of Christ, Whose Spirit is capable of guiding your kundalini energies toward a wholesome integration. Trust that a Higher Guidance is at work in the process. Ask for this Guidance when confused; listen for the answers.

8. Accept the pains that come and willingly cooperate with asanas and compulsions to meditate. These all pass away in time.

9. Practice yogic asanas for at least fifteen minutes a day to help facilitate the movement of the energy. Also consider using Tai Chi, massage, and/or movement therapies, especially when the energy seems to be blocked.

10. Learn to breathe abdominally.

11. Practice the *mahabandha lock* under the supervision of an experienced guide. Tuck the chin into the chest, thawing the navel inward and upward during exhalation while gently contracting the anal sphincter and perineal muscles. Keeping the chin tucked in, relax the muscles during inhalation drawing the navel outward to pull the diaphragm downward. Gently repeat this pattern of contracting and relaxing muscles while exhaling and inhaling deeply, attaching a spiritually focused mantra (e.g., "Come, Lord") to the breathing pattern.

12. Eat a balanced and nutritious diet, avoiding red meat, eggs, spicy foods, alcohol, coffee, and empty calorie sweets. Eat more fruit, vegetables, brown rice, grains, nutritious pastries, cheese, milk, yogurt, tofu, and nuts. These healthy foods probably do play a vital role in producing maximum nutrition and minimum pollution to a body undergoing physiological changes.

13. During times of strong energy upheavals, keep food in the stomach. A small snack such as bread and butter every three hours will help to minimize burning sensations in the stomach.

14. Avoid all forms of willful, competitive activities that generate fear and anger, for these will contaminate the energy with painful emotions.

15. Learn to deal with feelings as they arise through proper communication skills.

16. Males should be especially careful about sexual expression. Although the research on kundalini and sexuality is only in its infancy, the experiences of many (the author included) point up a definite relationship between kundalini energy and sexual energy. Genital sexuality should not be divorced from love, or else one's spiritual energy and physiological responsiveness will be lowered.

2.

Kundalini: The Big Picture

As a Christian and a Westerner, I have struggled to relate Eastern understandings of kundalini, chi energy, chakras, and even human nature to the traditional models I have been taught. It seems to me that this ought to be possible, however, for human nature is the same in both East and West, and indeed I am happy to report that a Western understanding of kundalini is possible. By "Western," here, I am referring primarily to the philosophical tradition that has moved from Aristotle through St. Thomas Aquinas to the neo-Thomistic theologians and philosophers of the late 20th C.[15]

In this chapter, I will reprint an essay written by Jim Arraj, who was a close friend and Thomistic scholar,[16] to introduce this Western way of understanding the place of kundalini in the spiritual life. Jim was one of several people who helped me identify what I was experiencing in the mid-1980s as kundalini, and we had many discussions and visits about this and other topics before his untimely death in 2009. In future chapters, we will reflect more deeply on the model he presents here, and relate it to a popular yogic understanding. I know it might feel as though one is jumping into the middle of a larger discussion, and that is indeed the case. But go ahead and dive in anyway, and

---

[15] E.g., Jacques Maritain and Jesuit Priests Teilhard de Chardin, Karl Rahner, and Bernard Lonergan. Worth mentioning here, too, is the tradition that moves through Philo and St. Augustine, and which has many parallels with the Thomistic approach.

[16] Jim Arraj was also a Catholic theologian, a scholar of Jung, and was deeply involved in Christian dialogue with Zen. The web site developed by him and his wife, Tyra, can be found at: http://innerexplorations.com

take your time to follow his line of reasoning. If you find it too difficult, just jump ahead to future chapters, then work your way back here.

A Christian Philosophical Explanation of Kundalini Energy
by James Arraj[17]

God and the intuition of being

St. Thomas Aquinas saw with an exceptional clarity into the very depths of things, into the heart of their being, and this insight Jacques Maritain, one of his greatest followers, later called the *intuition of being.*[18] We are intimately familiar with the differences among things. We say, "This is an apple." or "This is a rose." And we tend to take these differences as the deepest level of things, for they make things be what they are, or so it seems to us. But St. Thomas saw that it was possible to probe deeper. There was another fundamental aspect of things which was the *very fact of their existence.* No matter how different things are *they all exist.* He saw that the very differences, or *whats,* of things were certain *capacities-to-be,* to receive existence. Existence revealed itself to him as richer and denser than how it appeared in this or that thing. It was as if both the apple and rose manifested different faces of what it meant to exist. They existed but with a limited existence which was limited by their very nature which made them to be what they

---

[17] Reprinted with permission from Tyra Arraj.
Originally published on the Internet: http://innerexplorations.com/ewtext/some.htm

[18] All italicized words, phrases and sentences in this essay have been added to call special emphasis to them.

are, and these natures or *essences* could be seen as certain capacities for existence.

Once Thomas saw this the very depths of things became transparent to him, and shimmering in those depths was the mystery of existence itself. Existence as received and limited demanded existence unlimited and unreceived. All things pointed by their very being to existence as un-contracted by this or that limited capacity for existence which makes a thing to be what it is. This fullness of existence transcends all the limited things of our experience, and in this way it is no thing, not in the privative sense of nothing, but without the limits that come from being the existence of this or that thing. This intuition of being became the heart of St. Thomas' metaphysics, and it leads to a metaphysical contemplation in which all things point to the abyss of existence that we call God.

God as creator and end

Therefore all things are partial reflections of existence itself. They are a rainbow of creatures that come forth from the fullness of existence and are meant to find the fullness of their meaning and purpose by returning to God. How do we return? By becoming what we are most fully, for our deepest natural bond with God is our very being. *The more we are ourselves the more we are united to God.* God did not create us for God's own benefit, for God was already the fullness of existence. God did it for our sakes so we could enjoy existence: our own, that of all creatures, and God's. It takes the whole of creation to express as fully as possible the mystery of existence, and all creatures have as their deepest goal to return to God by achieving the full development and activation of their natures.

The ladder of being

Let's imagine, in a somewhat anthropomorphic way, God at work creating the universe. God decided it would be fun to see all the different kinds of things that could be made, starting with those closest to God's own nature, which would be the highest of purely spiritual beings. To be a pure spirit means to have an interior transparency of being that expresses itself in self-awareness and choice. As soon as God created these purely spiritual beings they immediately grasped themselves in knowledge and love. Their whole nature was present to them, and this was so true that God discovered that it was not possible to create more than one being at each rung of the ladder of being for each of these beings, because each one was purely spiritual, it filled up completely that certain kind of possibility so that there would be nothing to differentiate it from another creature of the same kind. Purely spiritual beings could only be one of a kind.

However, since spirit is very deep and rich, God was busy for a long time filling these spiritual rungs. But finally God was done, and since the process had been so enjoyable God looked around to see what to do next.

The human soul and the material universe

What to do next was a real puzzle. Was it possible to make something that was not spiritual? And even if it were, what would be the point, for or it would not truly know it existed and could not blossom in knowledge and love. God pondered this for a long time and then the inspiration came for a bold experiment. It was true that every rung in the ladder of spiritual beings was filled, but what if it were possible to use the bottom side of the lowest rung? The result would not be an active spiritual being — all those places were filled —but a new sort of spiritual being, one in potency to become a spiritual being. It would not have an immediately fully activated intellect, but a passive one that had the capacity to become activated. This idea created even more problems. What could activate it? It could not be the higher spiritual beings, for it did not have the capacity for such rich messages. It could not be itself for it was starting off in potency. God thought and thought and finally discovered a way out of this dilemma. What if the ladder of beings could be extended so that there could be an entirely new kind of being which was not spiritual, but found an ultimate expression in knowledge and love not in itself, but in virtue of its relationship with this new kind of spiritual being in potency, and this spiritual being, in turn, would be nourished by these other kinds of beings so that it could activate itself.

Whew! This posed a whole new set of problems. If a creature was not spiritual, then that meant its very essence or nature was such that it was not transparent to itself. It could not immediately become what it was meant to be, and it could never reach spiritual awareness. God saw that once the threshold of spiritual beings had been passed, then these new creatures would have a new kind of fundamental capacity to become what they were meant to be. Their natures or forms were too weak to immediately express and activate themselves. This was no longer the fundamental capacity that all things had by the fact that their natures were certain capacities for existence. This was a new kind of capacity, a capacity for the essence to become itself, to reach its own fullness of existence.

Matter, space and time

All this was very puzzling. God saw that creating this lowest spiritual being in potency was going to be quite a complicated matter. If it were to be stimulated in order to activate itself, it would need some sort of stimulus that was as active as possible and as close as possible in nature to it, something as digestible as possible, as it were. It would need the highest and most active form of this whole new class of non-transparent beings. Unfortunately, this highest form could not exist if it, in turn, were not aided to full development by the next highest form, for or it, too, was very much a being in potency to become what it was. And this next highest form demanded the one immediately below it, and so forth down the whole ladder of being. So God saw that it was necessary to start at the very bottom rung of the ladder and create the most elemental form of this new kind of being.

God created this kind of being and was amazed it was. By nature it had no capacity to be present to itself like spiritual beings did. It simply lacked the necessary ontological density. Therefore if it could not be part-less it had to express itself in part outside of part. It had to exist as a material body. And since it could not be all at once fully what it was meant to be it could not completely fill this lowest rung of the ladder of being. It needed other beings of identical nature to try to express what it meant to be this particular kind of thing. Thus was born a multiplicity of bodies, and the relationship between these bodies is what we call space. And all these bodies in virtue of their common nature were dynamically bound together and interacted and moved each other to realize their potential, and this change and motion are what gave rise to time.

In this way God created the material universe and inscribed in it was a primordial urge to reach up in ever greater complexity toward consciousness, which was its own way to return to God.

Stages in the journey

Naturally, St. Thomas in the 13th century did not know about evolution, but if he had I doubt he would have been disconcerted. He would have plotted the main stages of that journey something like this. First came the basic elements which arranged themselves into systems of greater and greater complexity, and after a very long time they reached the threshold of vegetative life. This life could not be the simple outcome of a random association of minerals but demanded, according to Thomas, a life principle or soul. He reasoned that life was more than being a body, for not every body is alive. There must be a vital principle that makes something be alive and organizes and directs that life. This new vegetative life had within it its own instinct to develop in the direction of greater self-awareness, and finally it reached the threshold of animal life with its motion and sense knowledge, rooted in an animal soul. Animal life, too, continued the long ascent toward genuine spiritual consciousness until it had reached the very threshold of the lowest of spiritual creatures. There was no way a material being could cross this threshold and give rise to spirit, for it was a different kind of being, but its own inner instinct had brought it to a peak of receptivity, and when this happened God infused in it the lowest of spiritual beings which is the human soul.

The union of body and soul

Finally, all the rungs of the ladder of being were filled. The creation of the lowest of spiritual beings had demanded the creation of the whole material universe. The human soul was at once the crown of this material universe and recipient of all its riches which it needed in order to activate itself. And it would be wrong to imagine that the human soul was somehow added to a physical body, a vegetative soul, and an animal soul as one more principle of organization or life. Its union with the universe was much more intimate than that. Thomas insisted that the human soul took up in itself and virtually contained these other principles. They were now contained within it in order that the unity of the human being would not be impaired. They became dimensions within the higher density of the spiritual soul and thus were present to it from within to help it activate itself. *Our bodies then in all their richness of elemental forms, vegetative life and animal awareness do not contain the soul, but rather they are contained in the soul.*

As human beings we straddle the very boundary that divides the universe into pure spirits and material beings. We possess the material part of the universe within us and it stimulates us to become aware of our spiritual natures, and the bond of being that unites us with all created things. The human soul is one of the strangest of creatures. It is spiritual but it is meant to be united with the whole universe through the body, and since it starts out as spiritual being in potency and is so united with material creation one soul does not fill its rung in the ladder of being. *A multitude of human beings are necessary in order to express what human nature is really like.* And because all human beings are partial expression of this same human nature, we are drawn to each other and are meant to help each other find full expression of what it means to be human.

Enlightenment[19]

We are now in a position to begin to create a Christian explanation of kundalini energy. The first step is to examine the nature of enlightenment itself, for kundalini appears to be a particular kind of enlightenment. We saw in Philip St.Romain's book that enlightenment is a direct non-conceptual seeing or awareness that I am and that all things are, that we all exist. It is an experience of the unity of things that they have in virtue of their existence, their common *isness*. In enlightenment there is an almost overwhelming sense of the oneness of things and our interior bond with all creation. Yet there is no explicit awareness of God as separate from this experience.

---

[19] In Chapter 1, I used the phrase "higher spiritual consciousness" as an alternative to "enlightenment," but am retaining the term here as it is what Jim Arraj used in his essay.

What is enlightenment from a Christian perspective? It is the counterpart to the intuition of being. If St. Thomas' metaphysical insight starts with the essence face of creation, the sense of the profound differences among things, and then works its way to their common isness, enlightenment bypasses this conceptual process. It is a direct perception of the existence face of creation. Everything is perceived just as it is with a vibrant richness and depth of being that comes from the very fact act that it exists, and this face of existence is the bond of unity among all things.

In the intuition of being we go conceptually from an understanding of essence as the source of difference to essence as a capacity for existence, and,the beings around us as limited and received existence to unlimited existence. We don't have an experience of this unlimited existence, but we see that all things in virtue of their very being demand its existence. In enlightenment non-conceptual means are used to experience the existence of things more deeply and directly. Everything is seen with the freshness in which it has come forth from the hand of God, but since there is no reasoning present, there is no explicit pointing to the existence of God. Rather, each thing shines from within with the infinite mystery of existence, and since this happens in a non-conceptual way it does not lend itself, in the experience itself, to reflection about the distinction between God and creatures.

While awareness of and reflection on the experience of enlightenment is new to Christians the intuition of being opens the way to do it. Enlightenment is the culmination of a natural process of development in which we experience our true natures as sharers in the mystery of existence, and as such it is a precious part of what it means to be a human being. It can only enrich Christianity and allow it to enter into deeper dialogue with those religions of Asia that hold this experience so much to heart. Enlightenment allows us to experience the wondrous mystery of existence that embraces all things, and as such it must be seen as the flowering of that instinct that is in all things to return to God by becoming what they were meant to be, and in the case of the human soul this instinct has blossomed into a spiritual experience of the highest intensity.

Kundalini as an integral form of enlightenment

Kundalini is meant to lead to enlightenment but it does so in a highly distinctive way, for it is a thorough-going activation not only of the mind but the body as well. From the Thomistic perspective we have just reviewed is it possible to make sense of this energy? Does such a process of development contradict what St. Thomas had to say about the union of soul and body? Not at all. Rather, they can mutually illuminate each other. *Kundalini is that fundamental energy or instinct of the soul that is inscribed in its very being which urges it to become fully alive and activated so that it can be and see its own existence and that of all things, and experience in them the radiant mystery of existence that we call God.* But if the human soul contains within it all the riches of elemental, vegetative and animal levels of existence, then this fundamental soul energy is animating all the levels of the human organism from within. But this presence of the soul is in some sense dormant, lying like a seed in these depths. In order to realize itself it must realize each and every level of its being. In short, *the human soul is the inmost animator by which these levels exist and by which they become activated.* In a certain way each of us contains the whole evolution of the material part of the universe, and our physical, psychological and spiritual growth is the activation of that heritage. Kundalini is not some strange freakish force coming from without, but it is a striking visible manifestation of an energy that is ceaselessly at work in all of us, both unconsciously and in our conscious strivings. Kundalini is the bursting forth of that soul energy that urges us to fulfill our destiny, but now becomes visible to us either because of our particular temperament or certain psychological gifts or traumas, or in response to some supernatural gift of God's grace. *The whole purpose of this energy is to make each level of our being, starting from the most elementary, fully alive and fully nourishing of the next highest level so that at the end of the process the deepest intuitive powers of the soul are awakened and we can see who we really are and that we are.* Kundalini can appear as an impersonal energy because it is not something under the control of the ego. It is very personal in the sense that it is an energy of the soul, but this energy must activate those levels of our being which are far from our conscious control. The human soul is present to the entire body, for it gives it existence. But its lower operations operate through various parts. The Hindu chakras and their associated nerve plexuses are fitting symbols of different levels that exist within the human soul. The traditional picture of kundalini lying dormant in the lowest chakra at the base of the spine is a fitting symbol of the human soul as a being in potency that needs to awake, and this is a process that proceeds from the bottom upwards, for the activation of the lower levels is necessary for the activation of the higher. And the activation of each level is the intensification of the powers belonging to each level and their orientation and transformation so they can best serve the human soul, which soul is deeper in them than they are in themselves, for it is what gives them existence. Further, in a highly analogous way, just as the soul is at the heart of these lower levels, God is at the heart of the soul giving it existence. Therefore, the more the soul experiences its own existence the more it is united to God even if in the actual experience the word God may not be used, for the experience happens non-conceptually. God is present in and through the existence of the soul which God constantly sustains.

Proceeding in this way, it would be possible to try to explain some of the other phenomena that are part of the kundalini process. If this energy is thwarted in its ascent by physical or psychological blocks it can cause physical pain and psychological disturbances. Its very activation will slow the mind's constant desire to conceptualize, preparing it for non-conceptual ways of seeing. The whole physical organism is activated in a new way leading to altered patterns of breathing and spontaneous gestures. And the psychological level of the soul is being transformed, as well, with alterations of the flow of psychic energy, the loss of affective memory, and so forth. And finally, the spiritual level of the soul, itself, is activated leading to the kind of seeing that is called enlightenment.

If these reflections are correct, at least in their general direction, then we stand at the beginning of a fascinating dialogue between the philosophy of St. Thomas and the natural phenomenon of kundalini, and through kundalini with those traditions which have studied it for so long. Thomistic philosophy can only be enriched by such a dialogue which would awaken it to its own resources which, in turn, could shed a new light on kundalini.

Conclusion

The key points for understanding kundalini from a Thomist perspective are the nature of the human soul as a spiritual being in potency which needs to be united to the material universe in the body in order to activate itself, and how the human soul contains and animates these lower levels of material being.

3.

A Closer Look

In our first chapter, we noted that the kundalini process is oriented toward the embodiment of higher spiritual consciousness, and in Chapter 2, Jim Arraj provided a cosmic context for understanding kundalini in terms of the soul and its full development. Later, we will examine more closely the nature of the energy involved, and why this process is often so difficult and painful. But first we need to focus more closely on human nature and define a few terms that we will be using in the rest of this book. I am convinced that this kind of understanding is in itself helpful unto the proper integration of kundalini, and also that lead to deeper self-knowledge as well.

Discussions of kundalini and chakras in the yogic literature usually present a view of the human in terms of multiple bodies, each of which serve as "containers" of sorts for certain potentialities. The most common presentation features five bodies:

1. *Gross Level.* The physical body and its senses.

2. *Vital Level.* Also called the Etheric body, this is the level that conducts the life force (prana, chi, etc.) to the physical body, producing physiological life in all its richness (digestion, excretion, reproduction, circulation, etc.). Acupuncture works with this level.

3. *Astral Level.* The body that contains and informs the previous two, and controls emotional life, desire, imagery and automatic thought processes.

4. *Intellectual Level.* The body that makes possible reason, intellectual life and conscience. It informs and orders levels 1 - 3.

5. *Causal Level.* Bliss body. Source of intuitive understanding, spiritual life, awareness.

Yogic disciplines focus on developing the full range of these human powers, with guidance on how to bring them into holistic integration. In order to do so, it is considered necessary to live moderately and to have a spiritual focus to one's life. Only such can bring enable one to harmonize Astral and Gross level potential with Causal life.

In the second edition of *Kundalini Energy and Christian Spirituality,* I included a detailed discussion of this yogic account in Appendix One, so I will not be going over that again here. As noted in Chapter 2, my greater interest in this book is to provide a Western context for understanding kundalini process, and I believe it is possible to do so using the approach outlined by Jim Arraj.

Human Nature

A common understanding in the West is that a human being is a composite of body and soul. The body is the material component, the soul is spiritual. At death, body and soul are separated, and in some religious traditions, it is believed that the soul lives on.

This is certainly easy to understand, but it leaves unanswered many questions. Where, for example, do we locate emotional life? Is that part of the body? The soul? Also, how do body and soul intercommunicate? And how are body and soul connected with God?

In Chapter 2, Jim Arraj introduced a model of human nature similar to the yogic bodies mentioned above. He noted:

> There must be a vital principle that makes something be alive and organizes and directs that life. This new vegetative life had within it its own instinct to develop in the direction of greater self-awareness, and finally it reached the threshold of animal life with its motion and sense knowledge, rooted in an animal soul. Animal life, too, continued the long ascent toward genuine spiritual consciousness until it had reached the very threshold of the lowest of spiritual creatures. There was no way a material being could cross this threshold and give rise to spirit, for it was a different kind of being, but its own inner instinct had brought it to a peak of receptivity, and when this happened God infused in it the lowest of spiritual beings which is the human soul.

We notice the word, *soul,* used here, and that a soul is a "vital principle that makes something alive and directs that life." Another way to think of it is that *a soul is the organizational intelligence that makes a creature be what it is.* In the case of the human, the soul is a "genuine spiritual consciousness," united with matter to form a living human body, which is necessary to activate the potential of the spiritual soul.

Arraj goes on to note that the human soul "contains" within itself vegetative (physiological) and animal (sensory, emotional) life, not as separate layers, but as potentialities available within the spiritual soul itself.

> Thomas insisted that the human soul took up in itself and virtually contained these other principles. They were now contained within it in order that the unity of the human being would not be impaired. They became dimensions within the higher density of the spiritual soul and thus were present to it from within to help it activate itself. *Our bodies then in all their richness of elemental forms, vegetative life and animal awareness do not contain the soul, but rather they are contained in the soul.* (Emphasis added.)

This understanding of the soul is most profound, and I have found that very few Christians are aware of this teaching. What Thomas and those who expounded on his work are saying is that:

- *It is the spiritual soul that constitutes the human as human*, governing the other levels (animal and vegetative) levels of our being. The soul is the organizational intelligence working in all the levels of our being to integrate and unify them.

- *The animal and vegetative levels exist for the soul to help activate and develop its intelligence.* The spiritual soul is not angelic, but is disposed toward union with both matter and God. A human without a body is thus metaphysically deficient.

- *A human being is an integrated whole*: an embodied soul, or enspirited body.

Some of this understanding has come into popular parlance as when, for example, we say that someone in a coma is in a *vegetative state*. This comes from the Aristotelian/Thomistic understanding of one the properties of vegetative souls — namely, to govern physiological life. In a comatose person, that's all you see, though the conviction remains that even in such a state, it is the spiritual soul that is responsible for the continuance of life. As long as the person is alive, the spiritual soul must still be connected with the body, for it is only at death that separation occurred. Likewise, we sometimes say that a person *acts like an animal*, behaving aggressively, lustfully, and/ or irrationally. In other words, such a person is giving evidence of the properties of the animal soul, without much evidence of rational life to check their impulsive behavior.

Proper to the life of the spiritual soul is *reason, or intellect,* a spiritual faculty that is inextricably connected with freedom and conscious awareness. This enables the human to not only adjust and respond to the environment as animals do, but to consciously and intentionally understand ourselves as the *subject* of knowing and action — a *self.* Intellectual life makes use of sensory and emotional data to activate its potential, then develops conceptual understanding that is one or more removes from the actual data itself. For example, humans naturally transition from the experience of a sweet-tasting fruit we name an "apple" to the concept of apple as a type of fruit that can be compared with other fruits. Once we move from the sensations of holding and eating the apple to thinking about it, we are actually experiencing the spiritual dimension of the soul, even though that might seem quite ordinary. We can begin to think about other things that have nothing to do with the sensate data — like maybe buying a bag of apples on the way home to make a pie to surprise someone. This thought triggers emotions of excitement and anticipation. We can then move on to thinking about that person and what we might say to them, which activates other feelings. This life of the mind is made possible by the spiritual soul, and we see how it informs and draws from the vegetative and animal levels within.

But what of God? If the soul is spiritual, is it "part" of God?

For St. Thomas and many other theologians in Christianity, the soul is not the same as God. It is a *creature,* and in the Judeo-Christian tradition that informed Thomas' thought, a creature is is not "part" of God, for God has no parts, but is purely spiritual and sufficient to Godself. The creature is to God as the artwork is to the Artist, or the word is to the Speaker. You cannot have a word without a Speaker, but the Speaker is not the word. Yet, there must be a relationship between Speaker and word for the latter wouldn't exist if it weren't Spoken in the first place, and the Speaking wouldn't have happened if there were no intent to manifest the word. Creation is thus completely dependent on God for its existence, but God is not dependent on creation for God's existence. This applies to the soul as well. It is a creation of God, not-God, and yet must have some connection with God in its act of existence or else it would cease to exist. Furthermore, God wills the human soul to exist, and that is why it exists and is a human soul rather than, say, a termite.

Another way of putting this is that the soul is *not-separate* from God, who is the Source of its existence, but it nonetheless is *distinct* from God, because it is something different from God — a creature. *Not-separate, but distinct:* it is important to hold these ideas together. This view recognizes the soul as a being that is *contingent* in that it depends on God for its existence. It also implies the existence of a kind of mystical "space," or *Ground of being,* wherein the soul is receiving its existence from God moment-by-moment. This Ground is sometimes called the A*pex* of the soul, and, as we shall see, it is unto this depth that the kundalini process is dynamically oriented.

A Modern Approach

During the past few decades, the philosophical approach of Thomism described above has often been replaced with terminology that resonates more with contemporary sciences. Regarding the body and its vegetative soul, Biology refers to the physical aspect of human life in terms of *organism*, which includes our anatomy and its physiological processes. Supplanting references to the animal soul, the science of Psychology refers to the *psyche*, with various methods for understanding emotional life, the unconscious realm, imagery, illnesses, and healing. The properties of the spiritual soul are sometimes included in the study of Psychology, but I will be following the method taken by Daniel Helminiak in referring to a dimension called *spirit* in reference to reason and freedom. Table 1 below compares these approaches with the yogic system of interpenetrating bodies described earlier in this chapter.

Yogic Sheaths	Thomistic Souls	Modern Approach
Gross	Body	Organism
Vital, Etheric	Vegetative	Organism
Astral	Animal	Psyche
Intellectual	Spiritual	Spirit
Causal	Ground of being, Esse	Ground of being, Apex

Table 1: Comparison of Yogic, Thomistic, and Modern approaches to human nature.

It is worth mentioning, here, that the Bible does not present a detailed, philosophical accounting of human nature, though it does, in places, use terminology similar to the modern approach. In 1 Thes. 5:23, for example, we read: "May God himself, the God of peace, sanctify you through and through. May your whole spirit, soul and body be kept blameless at the coming of our Lord Jesus Christ." The Greek term for "soul" here is "psyche," which corresponds to our use of this term as a level between spirit and body (while "soul" in this book is the formative spiritual intelligence). Rather than taking passages like this one as suggesting a biblical anthropology, it is probably best to view them in their context as a kind of "fullness of surrender" to God. The same goes for other passages, such as Jesus' saying we are to love God with our whole heart, soul, mind and strength. Jesus is not teaching us about human nature so much as to love God as fully as we possibly can.

The comparisons in Table 1 are not perfectly correlated, but they do serve to demonstrate similar insights into human potential and functioning. In all three systems, there is a physical/physiological level, a spiritual/rational level and an in-between layer that humans share with the animals. I am going out on a limb somewhat in suggesting that the yogic Causal Body is similar to the Western notions of Ground of being, Esse, or Apex, but I think there are similarities of experience to warrant this correlation. We will take up this consideration more fully in our next chapter on energy. One final point is that I will often use the term *level* in reference to these dimensions of human nature.

Table 2 below presents more extensive elaboration on the three modern levels:

		Experience	Needs	Disciplines
HUMAN BEING	**Spirit**	Self-Awareness Intellect Free-will	Authenticity Understanding Love Meaning	Theology Philosophy Spirituality The Arts
	Psyche	Temperament Imagery Memory Emotion	Be at peace Imagine, dream Remember Security, Belonging	Psychology Ethology
	Organism	Sensation Bodily Life	Eat, Rest Eliminate Waste Exercise, Sleep Clothing, Shelter	Physiology Biology Biochemistry

Table 2: Three Levels of Human Functioning

Figure 1 below is depicts the three levels in their relationships to each other:

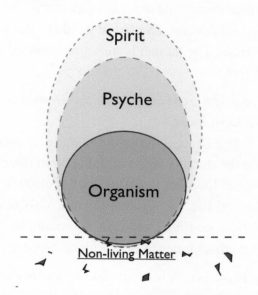

Figure 1: Three Levels of Human Nature

Note that the human spirit "contains" the levels of psyche and organism, and that psyche contains organism only. Dotted lines are intended to suggest that we are open to interaction with information from the physical, psychological and spiritual realms. We are not closed systems

A few principles help to explain basic interactions among the three levels.

1. *Lower levels are foundational for the higher ones.*
   Everything begins with sensory information (organism), for example, without which psychological and spiritual life can be developed. Likewise, psychological life informs spiritual activity, providing the affective context for determining meaning. This principle affirms a "bottom-up" dynamic for human development.

2. *A higher level informs and integrates the lower ones that exist within it.*
   The spiritual soul is the organizing principle for the levels of organism and psyche. They exist "within" the soul as part of human nature. The human is thus an embodied and en-psyched spirit.

3. *Lower levels still operate within higher ones according to their own lawfulness.*
   Like all living beings, we need to eat, drink, sleep, exercise and do all the things other mammals do to maintain bodily health. When the wise Socrates drank poison, it killed him. Psychological life, too, gives evidence of dynamics found in animals: fight-or-flight response, for example. There are appropriate disciplines to deal with all three levels.

4. *Damage to a lower level impedes the expression of a higher through it.*
   Psychological wounds skew spiritual functioning in humans. People with brain damage cannot do complex reasoning.

5. *Developmental factors constrain how much a higher level can manifest through a lower.* A baby cannot do algebra. A teenager needs to develop psychologically before accepting the responsibilities of marriage.

6. *Overly intensifying activities in one level diminishes manifestation through others.*
   It's as though the energy level at any given time is somewhat fixed, and so to transfer energy to one level means depriving others, at least for a short while. After eating a big meal, the digestive system needs more energy, so we feel lethargic for awhile. Too much mental activity can also wear down the body, as can worrying.

Kundalini Dynamics

Keeping this understanding of human nature and its intrapersonal dynamics in mind, we can return to Jim Arraj's essay in Chapter 2, and some of his comments about kundalini:

> But if the human soul contains within it all the riches of elemental, vegetative and animal levels of existence, then this fundamental soul energy is animating all the levels of the human organism from within. But this presence of the soul is in some sense dormant, lying like a seed in these depths. In order to realize itself it must realize each and every level of its being. . . In short, the human soul is the inmost animator by which these levels exist and by which they become activated.

Principles 1 and 2 described above resonate with this insight and point out the importance of doing one's work in terms of proper care of the body and psyche.

> The whole purpose of this energy is to make each level of our being, starting from the most elementary, fully alive and fully nourishing of the next highest level so that at the end of the process the deepest intuitive powers of the soul are awakened and we can see who we really are and that we are.

Principle 5 above affirms a natural unfolding of human development, and Jim's point introduces kundalini as an ordering principle that guides human development from the beginning. This broad understanding of kundalini can be found in some of the kundalini literature, and helps us to recognize kundalini activation as a further development of a process that is at work in us from conception onward: the kundalini dynamic.

> Kundalini can appear as an impersonal energy because it is not something under the control of the ego. It is very personal in the sense that it is an energy of the soul, but this energy must activate those levels of our being which are far from our conscious control.

The sense of kundalini as impersonal is troubling to many who experience an activation, as it feels different from divine consolations or psychological experiences. People sometimes wonder if they are possessed by a demon, and there are indeed cases where demonic influence is at work. But it is best, I believe, to consider kundalini to be a process originating in the unconscious, ever at work to grow us and awaken us to the fullness of human potential.

> Further, in a highly analogous way, just as the soul is at the heart of these lower levels, God is at the heart of the soul giving it existence. Therefore, the more the soul experiences its own existence the more it is united to God even if in the actual experience the word God may not be used, for the experience happens non-conceptually. God is present in and through the existence of the soul which God constantly sustains.

This insight is very important in that it locates kundalini in the Apex, or Ground of being, where the spiritual soul receives its existence from God moment-by-moment. It is thus a very special kind of energy, moving our development toward awareness of our inner connection with God. Nevertheless, it not God or the Holy Spirit as understood in Christian theology and spirituality, but is a "natural grace" inscribed in our being to lead us to God.

> Its very activation will slow the mind's constant desire to conceptualize, preparing it for non-conceptual ways of seeing. The whole physical organism is activated in a new way leading to altered patterns of breathing and spontaneous gestures. And the psychological level of the soul is being transformed, as well, with alterations of the flow of psychic energy, the loss of affective memory, and so forth. And finally, the spiritual level of the soul, itself, is activated leading to the kind of seeing that is called enlightenment.

> Principles 2, 3, 5 and 6.

Note here, too, that the term "enlightenment" is being used to describe the goal of the kundalini process. I have misgivings about this, as the term implies a certain spiritual "status" in some

Eastern and New Age circles, and is seldom used in the West. But it was one of Jim's burning desires to give an accounting of Eastern enlightenment in terms of Thomistic philosophy, and I think he has succeeded here as well as anyone I've ever read.

Finally, principle 3:

Proceeding in this way, it would be possible to try to explain some of the other phenomena that are part of the kundalini process. If this energy is thwarted in its ascent by physical or psychological blocks it can cause physical pain and psychological disturbances.

Would that we were all nice and clean and open as depicted in Figure 1, but the reality is more likely to resemble this:

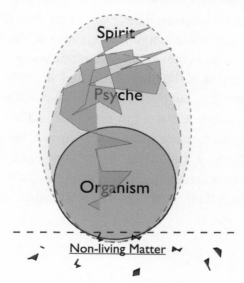

Figure 2: Wounded Human Nature

Every world religion recognizes the reality of human brokenness — that we all grow up in a world of conditional love, where we experience shame, rejection, neglect and abuse. To compensate, we recoil in fear and develop complicated, interlocking systems of defenses that impact all three levels of our human nature. Cleaning up our inner "mess" is important work that can entail counseling, journaling, forgiveness, meditation, etc. In almost every case of kundalini activation, however, one's brokenness will become painfully exposed, more so in certain individuals than others. A premature activation due to excessive meditative practices can be especially disruptive, as the energy cannot flow properly or attain its desired goal if embodied defenses skew its flow. Nevertheless, kundalini can also be a great ally unto healing, as it pushes its way through the human system, dismantling defenses, unblocking energy passageways, and prodding one to keep on going. In some strange way, as Jim Arraj has noted, the destination is embedded in the energy itself, and we can sense this even as we struggle.

But let us all be clear, here: even in the best of cases, integrating a kundalini activation is a very difficult process, and few there are who achieve this without ongoing issues. We can come to a place of sufficient healing and stability to live a healthy human life, but it will never be one that is devoid of struggle, and many will need to drastically adjust their lifestyle. The reason is that we are just too sick to ever become completely healthy, and if that weren't bad enough, the human cultures we have created keep dragging us down as well. God is present through it all, however, and can further help us to cope and find our way.

4.

Energies of the Soul

Let's begin by considering a steam-powered locomotive engine. The engineer shovels coal into a firebox of burning coal, and this heat is used to boil water, which produces steam to power the engine that turns the wheels. If asked what makes the locomotive run, many would respond that it is the burning coal, but that answer would be inadequate. The energy is what powers the *system of intelligence* we call a locomotive engine, which is precisely designed to convert the steam to mechanical energy to power its engine. Apart from this intelligence, the burning coal simply heats up the air and water; without the heat, the locomotive just sits there.

This is a good way to understand a living thing as well, including humans. Our energy comes from the food we eat and the air we breathe (indirectly, from the sun; ultimately, from the Big Bang). But clean air, water and food sitting on a table do not produce the energy that we call life. What is required is an exquisite system of interrelated organ systems to metabolize the food into energy that feeds our cells, powers our muscles, and provides electricity for our nervous system. The biological sciences have come to a deep understanding of how the human organism is energized and how it functions. We know, too, that the coordination of these processes is complicated, involving the brain, genes, endocrine glands, and numerous feedback dynamics. But what is it that integrates all these parts and functions into one coordinated whole? In response, we can say that *it is the human soul that does so.* Even if science were to provide a complete accounting for how the body functions as an integrated unit, the term, *soul*, as a philosophical designation for this coordinating intelligence, would still be valid.[20]

We spoke of the soul in previous chapters, and here we see its relationship to matter and energy. You don't find something called generic matter anywhere; matter is always of a particular type, whether living or inert.[21] What makes matter to be one type and not another is its *form*, which is what constitutes it with particular properties.[22] Likewise, the soul is held to be the *form of the body*, which is to say that a human organism is human because it has a human soul, or form. In some mysterious manner, body and soul are united to create one unit, an individual human being. The term for this is *hylomorphism*, and we alluded to it in the previous chapter by noting that a human is an embodied soul, or, conversely, and enspirited body. It is not a body that smiles and walks and reads books; it is an embodied soul that does so.

Can science prove the existence of the human soul?

No. A soul is not some-thing that can be measured or experimented with, but refers to the *integrative intelligence and principle of life* that makes all the levels of our human nature work as one unit. As with the intelligence that makes a steam engine work, it is itself invisible, but its influence is observable in the matter that it organizes and animates — the body.

---

[20] Daniel Siegel's discussions of the mind resonate with this understanding. See *Mind: A Journey to the Heart of Being Human* (New York, NY: W. W. Norton & Co., 2017)

[21] Aristotle and the Thomists did speculate on matter without form, calling it "primary matter," but could provide no specific examples of such. It was more of a philosophical hypothetical.

[22] This explanation of form is from the Aristotelian, Thomistic philosophical tradition.

What of energy, then?

As noted above, biology can explain much about how the body is energized by food, water and oxygen. Emerging from these processes is a new kind of energy — *life* — something entirely new, unexpected, and difficult to explain. It cannot be found apart from the molecules and chemical reactions that undergird it, but it also seems to coordinate these activities to maintain itself — and here we can suggest that it does so through the organizational intelligence of the soul. *Life is thus of the soul and the body, and is the energy that relates body and soul to each other.*

When the organ systems of the body can no longer maintain the processes necessary to sustain life, the body dies, and, in some sense, the soul does as well. It can no longer develop itself through a living body as is its natural disposition. Apart from the soul to maintain its overall form and integration, the body becomes a corpse and begins to fall apart . . . to de-compose. But what of the pattern of intelligence that made the body into a living thing? Does it survive apart from the body? Again, science cannot say, as this is outside its province. Phenomena like near death experiences are suggestive and can be investigated by scientists, but stories of such are anecdotal and impossible to corroborate.

In many Christian denominations, it is held that the soul, at death, continues to exist, only in a state of metaphysical deficiency. Apart from the body, it cannot develop its powers or exercise itself, so its development and moral/spiritual attitude is "fixed," at death. "As the tree falleth, so it lies in eternity," goes the old saying. The soul continues in existence, yearning to be united with a body for completion. Eastern religions posit a re-incarnation of a soul to continue its journey, but such belief has been formally rejected in Christianity several times. For one thing, it is difficult to understand how the pattern of intelligence achieved by the soul during its time of embodiment can be transferred to another body. What Christians believe instead is that the risen Christ has provided this new Foundation for the soul and provided a new life, *Zoe,* to sustain it.

Bios - Biological Life

In chapter 3, we referred to levels of human experience and noted parallels between yogic, Thomistic and modern approaches to understanding these levels. Table 1 compared these to each other, and now we are returning to these levels to help us better understand life energy and how it works in a human being.

The first level in the modern approach (levels one and two in the yogic and Thomistic) has to do with the body and its physiological processes. It is not a separate layer as, say, a first-stage rocket booster engine, but is a dimension within the soul itself. As principle #3 in chapter 3 noted, it operates according to its own lawfulness in a manner like that of other animals, especially the more advanced mammals. From them, we have inherited the genetic intelligence to metabolize food, water and air into energy that flows through a living body, or organism. *Bios* is the traditional Greek word used to describe this energy, and it is even found in the Bible in reference to God's gift of physical life to creatures.[23]

Evidence of bios in an organism is that it breathes, digests food, circulates blood, excretes waste, sleeps, procreates — all the things animals do as well. A body that has just died looks much the same as it had a few seconds before, only there is no longer any bios. Sometimes, as we noted in Chapter 3, when a

---

[23] Acts 17:28, "For in him we live and move and have our being."

person is comatose, we say they are in a vegetative state; there is still evidence of bios, but not much else.

In accord the principle #1 in Chapter 3, the life of the body is foundational to the soul and its operations. That life, bios, is primarily oriented to sustaining the life of the body, but it also moves toward providing energy and information to the higher levels of psyche and spirit. These, in turn, can influence its functioning. *The flow of life in a human being is both up and down and all-around,* and there are many factors that affect this flow. We'll say more about this later. For now, the main point is that bios is our most basic human energy — the steam, as it were, that powers the human locomotive.

Table 2 notes several disciplines that study the level of organism and its bios: biology, biochemistry, and physiology are mentioned. Allopathic medicine also focuses on the organism and its functioning, and has made amazing advances to promote health and healing of the body. Disciplines such as proper diet, exercise and sleep help to maintain biological health, which is necessary to produce and sustain bios. When bios is weak, psyche and spirit will be affected as well, so it is good to do all one can to properly care for the body. Spiritualities in the East and West emphasize this point most strongly.[24]

Of all the different energy processes that contribute to bios, sexual energy, or *libido*, is most significant, as it is specifically ordered toward bringing forth new life. This energy is also a major factor in kundalini process, as it seems to be "taken up," as it were, to be used to power higher levels of human

---

[24] Lee Sannella's book, *The Kundalini Experience*, investigates what he calls the physio-kundalini process. Jana Dixon's *Biology of Kundalini* (also a web site) provides extensive study of how biological factors influence the kundalini process, and vice versa.

consciousness and functioning.[25] That is why it should not be wasted through masturbation and excessive sexual activity, as these diminish an essential source of what shall become spiritual energy.[26]

Psuche: Psychological life[27]

As we move from lower to higher animals, we find evidence of another kind of life that is not simply physiological. This level of life in a human is called *psuche,* and it is the the word from which psychology is derived. It is characterized by a more highly developed functioning of the senses, capacity for movement, emotional experience, and instinctive drives. This is accompanied by the development of a more complex brain.

Psuche is not separate from bios, but is derived from it; the two merge and blend and inform one another. In some schools of psychology, it is held that libido is deeply influential of psychological life. In the animals, it moves the body to help meet basic needs, but it also has new concerns like establishing territory, dominance hierarchies, migration, responding to danger, attracting a mate, raising young, and even play. Because we humans also experience this kind of life, we often feel a bond of closeness to certain animals, and we value our pets. They truly can be a source of emotional companionship.

---

[25] There are numerous teachings about this in various Eastern systems, which describe a subtle energy derived from the reproductive fluids that is essential for overall health.

[26] It may well be that this dynamic is one of the primary reasons why celibacy is recommended for those in consecrated religious life.

[27] The term, *psuche,* is an alternate spelling of the Greek word, *psyche.* For purposes of this work, I will use psuche in reference to the energy, and psyche in reference to the level of human nature.

But psuche in a human is not the highest life; it is a kind of middle-ground between biological and spiritual life, which makes use of psuche to provide a dimension of affective responsiveness and symbolic meaning. Whereas emotions in animals are an inner barometer to help them evaluate their environment, in humans they also become guides to help evaluate the *meaning* of life events. Psychology works with this level to help us heal from repressed emotions, traumatic experiences, and to understand our natural temperamental dispositions.

What happens to psuche when an animal dies? Traditionally, it was held that this level had not crossed the threshold to spiritual life, and so it dissipated along with the body at death. But who really knows?

Psuche is very much involved in the kundalini process, as it needs to become purified of negative emotions and self-serving desires. Proper care for the psyche is of great value, of course, whether or not one undergoes a kundalini activation. Disciplines like journaling, examining attitudes, working on relationship skills, emotional awareness and dreamwork can help one to live more fully at this level.

Pneuma - Spiritual Life

Somewhere, somehow, during the long journey of mammalian evolution, a new kind of life emerged that we call *pneuma*. The term can mean breath, wind, or spirit, and it is conceptually similar to the Hebrew term *ruah*. In the New Testament, it is sometimes used to refer to the Holy Spirit, which is divine, or to the human spirit, which is created by God. I will capitalize the term when referring to God. What I am referring to here is human spiritual life.

Pneuma is the energy that powers our spiritual consciousness. Working through a more complex brain, it is a further refinement of bios and psuche, which it makes use of in producing a new type of knowing that seems to be unique to humans. Pneuma energizes bios and psuche so they not only function according to their own lawfulness, but as information sources within the field of living consciousness that pneuma radiates. We can think, reason, deliberate options, predict outcomes, and, through it all, be aware of ourselves as the subject of these spiritual processes — a self. Pneuma also has a top-down influence on our psychological and biological functioning, as it is the medium in which thoughts occur, and thoughts influence feelings, digestion, heart rate and many basic functions. Likewise, it is weakened to some degree when the body and psyche are suffering.

Obviously, pneuma is a very special energy, and one that needs to be properly cared for. Because it takes a great deal of bios and psuche to power pneuma, we need to sleep, at times, to take breaks, to let our energies balance out and become refreshed. Over-doing it through too much mental concentration, for example, will ultimately deplete the energies of the lower levels. This is in accord with principle #6 that we shared in Chapter 3, something I experience when I read for too long, or when I work work too much on a writing project. It might be fun and stimulating while I'm in the midst of it, but eventually there is diminishment. Usually, there are signals from the body and psyche that one needs to take a break, but these can be ignored, usually causing problems, to some degree.

In addition to its top-down influence noted above, pneuma is also naturally oriented toward transcendence — that there are "higher" realms to wonder and think about. Adaptation to earthly life is a large part of its concern, of course, but pneuma also empowers the soul to develop its intellectual potential to seek ultimate truth, meaning and love. It gives rise to new disciplines like philosophy and theology, and expresses itself through the arts as well. Pneuma can also become corrupted and debased through poor choices and addictive involvements; it can also become attached to accumulating power. Spiritual light and darkness are possible outcomes for pneumatic development. Healthy pneuma is open to transcendence and accepting of life in a body on Earth.

There is much more that could be said about bios, psuche and pneuma, but the general descriptors provided above will suffice for now. Figure 3 below images these in terms of the three levels of human nature pictured in Figure 1.

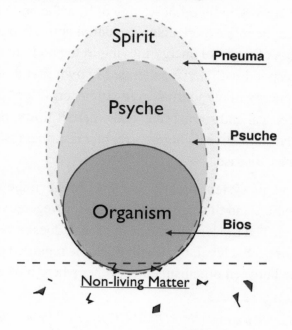

Figure 3. Three Kinds of Life

The Vital Interface

In addition to the three levels of intelligence and life described above, Table 1 lists a level between organism and psyche that the yogic system calls the Vital or Etheric Body. This is the level through which energy flows along meridians that acupuncturists have learned to work with. This energy is called *chi* in the Chinese system and *prana* in Hinduism, and seems to be referring to the same phenomenon.

The Western approach I have described does not have a precise equivalent for the Vital Body. Indeed, all of the reading I've done about this situates it in the context of a vitalist cosmology with which the West is mostly unfamiliar.[28] And yet, it's obvious from the successes achieved by acupuncturists in helping to relieve pain and restore health that there is a real wisdom at work in their knowledge of how the body is energized. People experiencing kundalini activation also report awareness of flows of energy moving in the body in ways that do not correspond with nerve patterns. My own first designations for this energy in my journal were "life energy" or "pure life." It feels electrical and stimulating, and where it flows, one is definitely more alive. Where it gets blocked, there is pain and, sometimes, disease.

The yogic system situates this level between the gross and astral bodies, and this corresponds with the vegetative soul in Thomism. The modern, tripartite approach does not explicitly recognize such a level, but it still could be regarded as an interface between organism and psyche, where bios and psuche

---

[28] *The Holy Spirit and Ch'i (Qi): A Chiological Approach to Pneumatology,* by Koo Dong Yun, is an attempt to relate Eastern understandings of energy to Christian teachings on the Holy Spirit. I found parts illuminating, but struggled with others.
- William Johnson, in *Mystical Theology: The Science of Love* (New York, NY: HarperCollins, 1995) included discussion of Eastern ideas on energy in a book that is largely about Christian mystical experience.

intermingle. In cases of kundalini process, it is where we experience intensely stimulated bios moving through the body to cleanse the tissues and bring the levels of human nature into alignment with the Ground of being. Eastern systems with wisdom concerning the dynamics of energy flow at this level can help us to integrate kundalini.

The Causal Body - Ground of Being, or Apex

Table 1 also indicates another level, called the Causal Body in the yogic system. This body is purely spiritual and knows intuitively rather than reflectively. When one is awake at this level, one experiences deep joy and peace. In some of the literature, it seems to be the level of the Atman, or indwelling divine; in others, it is the final veil before realizing the Atman.

A similar idea in Western spirituality can be found in the idea of the Ground of Being, or Apex. The theologian, Paul Tillich, wrote of this, as did the transpersonal psychologist, Michael Washburn. Christian mystical writers have spoken of this Ground as a kind of interface between God and the human — the inner "place" where existence is received from God moment-by-moment. It is also sometimes called the Apex of the soul. Catholic monk Thomas Merton writes of this experience:

> At the center of our being is a point of nothingness which is untouched by sin and by illusion, a point of pure truth, a point or spark which belongs entirely to God, which is never at our disposal, from which God disposes our lives, which is inaccessible to the fantasies of our own mind or the brutalities of our own will. This little point of nothingness and of absolute poverty is the pure glory of God in us... It is like a pure diamond, blazing with the invisible light of heaven. It is in everybody, and if we could see it we would see these billions of points of light coming together in the face and blaze of a sun that would make all the darkness and

cruelty of life vanish completely...I have no program for this seeing. It is only given. But the gate of heaven is everywhere.[29]

Spiritual author and theologian, Carla Mae Streeter, OP notes the following:

This depth or height is the point of entry and indwelling of God's self-gift in love. . . It (the idea of the Apex) appears in the writings of the early mystics and often takes on the rich imagery of the history of the time of its use. Catherine of Siena refers to the "cell" of the heart. Teresa of Avila speaks of the "innermost room of the castle" to refer to this inner point of divine encounter. . . They (the mystics) describe a hidden depth where the Divine is found shrouded in the darkness or opaqueness of faith in the midst of mundane activities.[30]

Michael Washburn describes this inner dimension as the Dynamic Ground in his book on transpersonal psychology.

The Dynamic Ground is the seat of the physico-dynamic pole of the psyche and the source of psychic energy. As such, it is the *sine qua non* of any kind of psychic functioning or conscious life. Experience in general is possible only on the assumption that there is a line of contact to the power that resides in, and flows from, this source.[31]

When it comes to levels of being and energy, the highest is also the most interior and even the source or cause of the functioning of the other levels. This is true of the Ground as well. It is the most interior depth of the soul, and, simultaneously, the ultimate source and influence over all the

---

[29] Thomas Merton, *Conjectures of a Guilty Bystander* (New York, NY: Image Books, 1968)

[30] Carla Mae Streeter. *Foundations of Faith A Systematic Approach* (Collegeville, MN: Michael Glazier Press, 2012). p. 61.

[31] Washburn's "psyche" is a combination of what we are calling spirit and psyche. See Michael Washburn. *The Ego and the Dynamic Ground: A Transpersonal Theory of Human Development* (Albany, NY: State University of New York Press, 1988).

other levels. Hence, the Ground, though spiritual, is also the source of the body, psyche and spiritual levels of being. It is from this depth that our existence emerges, and unto this depth that our energies are ultimately aligned. We generally lose touch with this through worldly concerns, addictions, attachments, etc., but through prayer, meditation, moral living and other spiritual practices, we begin to feel our growth being drawn unto this depth.

I am OK calling the Causal Body or Ground another level of human nature primarily to distinguish it from what we have called the spiritual level and its ordinary functioning. In reality, however, I think the human spirit itself opens naturally unto the Ground, which is why I have not indicated the Ground as a separate level in the pictorial images I have provided. If I were to do so, it would be on the outer boundary of the spiritual level, as an interface between the spirit and the divine. But it is also the interface between everything else that exists in us as well, and I have no idea how to depict that. As Washburn noted in a different work, "it has roots that reach into the neurological strata" and is thus "unfathomable in its depths."[32]

Zoe - Divine Life

For the sake of completion, we need to mention *Zoe*, which I will capitalize, as it often refers in the New Testament to divine life -- life to the full.[33] As such, it is not an energy or life that is natural to humans, but which is shared with us by God as gift. When Zoe is strong in a soul, it rightly orders the functioning of

---

[32] Michael Washburn, *Embodied Spirituality is a Sacred World*, p. 221. (Albany, NY: State University of New York Press, 2003), p. 221.

[33] See John 10:10

pneuma, psuche and bios. When one lives willfully, Zoe is weakened and there is disorder in our natural energies.

In Christian understanding, the presence of Zoe can be recognized through the fruits of the Spirit: "love [unselfish concern for others], joy, [inner] peace, patience [not the ability to wait, but how we act while waiting], kindness, goodness, faithfulness, gentleness, self-control."[34] Zoe also brings healing, wholeness, and deepens our human capacity for knowing and understanding.

> For what person knows the thoughts and motives of a man except the man's spirit within him? So also no one knows the thoughts of God except the Spirit of God. Now we have received, not the spirit of the world, but the [Holy] Spirit who is from God, so that we may know and understand the [wonderful] things freely given to us by God.[35]

Zoe is the sacred yeast that ferments our human energies unto the image and likeness of God we were created to be.[36] It is the role of religion to orient us toward the divine and teach us how to become more open to accepting and co-operating with Zoe. Spirituality provides the practices that enable us to do so.

Kundalini Energy

Finally, we are in a position to speak of kundalini energy. For some writers, no distinction is made between kundalini and

---

[34] Gal. 5:22-23. Amplified Bible.

[35] 1 Cor. 1:11-12. Amplified Bible.

[36] This process is called theosis, or sanctification.

Zoe.[37] I disagreed with this in my earlier book, and will here continue to make a distinction between the two. What is obvious, however, is that for many, kundalini activation happens in the context of spiritual practice and a deep devotion to God, with abundant signs of Zoe manifesting during the course of the process. It's kind of a "chicken-and-egg" situation: which one accounts for the other? That is not always the case, however, which is why I make the distinction. While growth in Zoe might indeed be the catalyst for kundalini awakening, this need not always be the case, and, at any rate, it is possible to distinguish kundalini phenomena even in the context of mystical infusions. After all, we would not say that the joyful feelings stirred by Zoe *are* Zoe, but would identify them as psychological in nature. In a similar manner, we can do the same with regard to kundalini.

What I am inclined to say, after all these years, is that kundalini is not Zoe, nor is it even another unique type of human energy found along with bios, psuche and pneuma. Rather, *kundalini is a more intensified experience of bios* flowing through the body to purify and heal the body, psyche and spiritual parts of our nature so that we might live in deeper alignment with the Ground of our Being, where the "gate of heaven" mentioned by Merton above opens to the inflow of Zoe.

Because the human soul is always naturally oriented toward the creation outside and the Ground within, the kundalini dynamic is always at work in everyone, to some extent. What we call kundalini activation is the *intensification* of the process —

---

[37] "Almost every tradition speaks of Kundalini in one form or another and describes Kundalini in its own way. In Japanese it is called *ki*; in Chinese, *chi*; the scriptures of Christianity call it the Holy Spirit. What is that Kundalini? It is the power of the Self, the power of Consciousness."
- Swami Muktananda. *Kundalini: The Secret of Life* (New York, NY: SYDA Foundation, 1979).

an ignition, as it were — hopefully in one who is prepared for what will be required. Our next two chapters will go more deeply into this.

5.

The Chakra System

The term, *chakra,* means wheel, or circle, and usually refers to energy centers found along the spine. They roughly correlate with nerve plexuses, but not precisely, for they exist in the yogic bodies between the physical and the spiritual levels. Some systems also relate the chakras to endocrine glands. The common teaching is that during a kundalini process, the chakras are stimulated and their powers enhanced, but first they must be cleansed of impurities. The Hindu system treats of seven major chakras and numerous minor ones; other spiritual systems describe more, or less. The number isn't all that important.

How might we understand chakras in the Western context presented thus far? One finds nothing about this in the writings of St. Thomas Aquinas and those who continued to develop his philosophy. However, Christian artists through the ages have alluded to energy centers remarkably similar to the yogic chakras. One will find pictures of Jesus, Mary, and Saints, for example, with light emanating from the forehead, heart, throat, and around the head — a halo. I doubt these artists were using Hindu metaphysics as a basis for their depictions, but they were intuitively expressing something about holiness and energy flow.

There are several ways to approach the topic of chakras in relation to kundalini process:

1. They are transformation stations that move energy through the various yogic bodies or levels of human nature — metaphysical organs, of sorts. Some authors describe them in

detail — their color, shape, sounds associated with, even markings that occur on them. [38]

2. As an approach to organizing teachings on the spiritual life. Carolyn Myss' best-selling book, *Anatomy of the Spirit: The Seven Stages of Power and Healing*,[39] comes to mind, here.

3. As a way of speaking about how different motives of attention are embodied.

4. As powers, or developmental potentialities of the embodied soul.

The approach I will take in this chapter will be mostly along the lines of #2 and 3, with #4 in mind as well. It is not so much that I dispute all the information taken in the first approach, but that I have no experience to corroborate it one way or the other. There may indeed be real energy organs that can be evaluated by people who have the psychic equipment to do so, but I am not one of them, nor have any of the hundreds of people I've been in dialogue with about kundalini shared anything about that. There are unquestionably places in the body where energy gathers, however, as in the heart, throat, forehead, and top of head, and that may well be because of metaphysical chakras. But I prefer to speak of these experiences in terms of approach #3 — how different motives of attention are embodied. Perhaps it is the chakras described in the yogic system that are involved with this, but even if there are no such things, it is a useful way to denote and describe such experiences.

---

[38] http://download.audible.com/product_related_docs/ BK_TANT_006589.pdf
See also the table on page 70 in the 2010 paperback edition of my book, KSP.

[39] Three Rivers Press, 1996

In the context of approach #3, we will explore the following points:

A. Attention is energetically embodied

B. Different motives of attention are embodied differently

C. Habitual attentiveness of a particular motive creates imbalanced embodiment and energy

D. Spiritual growth entails bringing the lower chakras into alignment with the higher.

A graphical depiction of the chakras using the model we have pursued thus far is presented below:

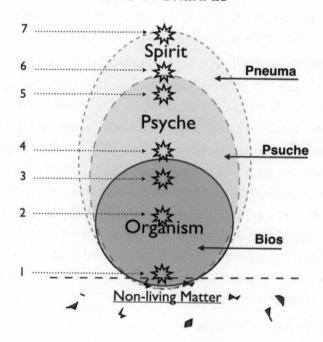

The 7 Chakras

Figure 4. The Chakras

A. Attention is Energetically Embodied

In Chapter 4, we noted that pneuma is the energy of human spiritual consciousness, which interacts with psuche and bios. As the old saying goes, a human being is an embodied soul, and our reflections on the energies give us an idea of how this works. In speaking of attention, here, we are recognizing that consciousness is not static, but can be focused by the will and intellect to concentrate pneuma in a particular direction. In my book, *God and I: Exploring the Connections Between God, Self and Ego,*[40] I called this *reflecting consciousness*, in contrast with *non-reflecting consciousness*, which is more unfocused, relaxed and open. Attention, then, is reflecting or intentional consciousness; awareness is open or non-reflecting consciousness. Awareness is the wider field within which attention is exercised.

Everything that happens to a human being happens in the body — even our highest, most exalted thoughts and mystical experiences. During the past few years, scientists have deeply explored the connection between consciousness and the body. We know that thoughts, which belong to the realm of spirit, influence our emotions, which belong to the level of psyche, and that emotions influence endocrine glands and various bodily responses. The primitive, mammalian fight-flight response can be triggered by thoughts such as, "what if they don't like me?" or "what if I get fired?" So well established is this relationship between consciousness and the body that we have long alluded to it in common expressions:

I have butterflies in my stomach
She gives me a pain in the neck

---

[40] Philip St. Romain. *God and I: Exploring the Connections Between God, Self and Ego* (Raleigh, NC: Lulu Press, 2016).

I was frightened speechless
My heart is on fire with love

Psychologists have recognized a variety of psycho-somatic illnesses, and mental stress is considered a drag on the immune system. Massage therapists help to release energy that has become stuck in the body's tissues. On the positive side, positive, affirming thoughts can give our emotional experience a boost. Athletes envision themselves performing well before a game, and it does seem to help. Attention is like a spiritual muscle that we can learn to exercise for good or for ill. Taking responsibility for how one gives attention to one's inner life and outer circumstances is a first and major step toward growth and healing.

B. Different Motives of Attention are Embodied Differently

Illustrations of the chakras like the one in Figure 4 usually show them strung like beads from the base of the spine to the top of the head. Different powers and needs are ascribed to each chakra, sometimes more in the interest of approach #2 on pedagogy mentioned above, it seems, though not entirely. If I were to ask where you feel sexual attraction in your body, the answer would probably be in the genital area. The desire for power and control is often felt in the solar plexus, tender feelings of love in the heart, the impulse to communicate in the throat area, and so forth. These associations are common enough to have merit, though they might not stand up to scientific scrutiny. But the main point is that various motives of attention resonate in different parts of the body, and I don't think that's controversial.

Table 3 provides a summary of associations between chakras, endocrine glands and motives of attention.

Chakra	Motive	Body Center	Endocrine
7	Pride	Mental	Pineal
6	Intuition	Forehead	Pituitary
5	Communicate	Throat	Thyroid
4	Love	Heart	Thymus
3	Power	Solar Plexus	Adrenals
2	Pleasure	Genitals	Leydig
1	Security	Base of Spine	Gonads

Table 3: Chakras and Motives

Readers familiar with developmental theorists like Maslow, Erickson, and Kohlberg will surely note a similarity between these chakra concerns and those articulated by the theorists. The concerns of all of the chakras are in play throughout life, but developing a mastery over these does seem to proceed in a certain order, from the bottom up, with the lower providing an infrastructure of sorts for the higher. The 6 principles from Chapter 3 that describe the interactions between higher and lower levels come into play as well, and I will list them here again for convenience. In place of the term "level," you can substitute "chakra" if you'd like.

1. *Lower levels are foundational for the higher ones.*

2. *A higher level informs and integrates the lower ones that exist within it.*

3. *Lower levels still operate within higher ones according to their own lawfulness.*

4. *Damage to a lower level impedes the expression of a higher through it.*

5. *Developmental factors constrain how much a higher level can manifest through a lower.*

6. *Overly intensifying activities in one level diminishes manifestation through others.*

C. Habitual Attentiveness of a Particular Motive Creates Imbalanced Embodiment and Energy

Energy flow follows attentional direction, and if one habitually attends to life a certain way, then energy will flow in a corresponding manner, influencing the body as it does so. For example, if one spends a great deal of time with pornographic material, there will be a disproportionate intensification of energy in the 2nd chakra. The same holds true for other motives and concerns, including developmental ones. There are indeed times in life when the lessons to be learned seem associated with certain themes and motives, beginning as toddlers with the lower chakra concerns and proceeding up the ladder as we age. Successful resolution of developmental issues allows for a freer flow of energy in the body; developmental wounds can restrict energy flow.

Thought focuses attention. The relationship between energy, attention and thought has long been noted by philosophers, theologians and spiritual writers. A 4th C. Christian monk named Evagrius wrote about eight predominant thoughts that accounted for human unhappiness: gluttony, greed, sloth, sorrow, lust, anger, vainglory, and pride. Through history, this list has been slightly altered, the result being what we call the Seven Deadly Sins. These are all consequences, to some degree, of developmental frustrations, but we can also encourage them ourselves. To the extent that we give attention to them, these thoughts become more intensified — more imbued with energy, and more embodied. Eventually, we are bound to act them out somehow if they are not checked and disciplined by liberating virtues, which are also thoughts we can meditate on and put into action: chastity, temperance, charity, diligence, patience, kindness, humility, and others. Table 4 below contrasts these and other deadly sins and redeeming virtues in light of chakra motivations.

Chakra	Deadly Thoughts	Disease	Liberating Virtue
7	Pride	Mental	Abandonment
6	Cynical, Dogmatic	Eye	Openness, Humility
5	Dishonest	Throat, Lungs	Honesty
4	Sorrow, Selfishness	Heart	Love
3	Anger, Envy	Digestive	Courage, Patience
2	Lust, Gluttony	Reproductive	Temperance, Chastity
1	Greed, Sloth	Lower Back	Trust

Table 4: Chakra Vices and Virtues

The diseases associated with the deadly thoughts are not a scientific listing, but generalizations on how the body holds energy. Holistic health practitioners use these kinds of considerations to point out psycho-spiritual factors that influence our health. Pneuma and its thoughts, psuche and its emotions: both influence bios, which in turn energizes the body. So, for example, if the heart is weak, one would be encouraged to become less selfish and more loving — practices that are beneficial no matter what a cardiologist might diagnose. The reasoning here is sound, but is not intended to present a tool for self-diagnosis and treatment, much less a weapon to use to justify blaming oneself for illnesses. Good and loving people have heart disease, and many greedy people have good backs. But if we really do believe that the body is more than a machine, and that thoughts influence the body, there is really a wisdom expressed in the chakra system and the light it sheds on health and disease.

Tables 3 and 4 also provide a sketch for using the chakra system in the service of teaching about the spiritual life. This teaching would elaborate more on points A, B and C above, and go into each of the chakras in terms of its body-center, motives, endocrine association, deadly thoughts, diseases, and liberating virtues. Additionally, such teaching could associate the chakras with the teachings of various developmentalists and add additional features like meditative practices to energize each. At a conference on kundalini issues I attended years ago, one of the teachers used the chakras to teach on the seven rooms in St. Teresa's interior castle. I'm not sure how well that worked out, but it did go to show how the chakras can provide a framework for teaching on spiritual practice — a topic that goes beyond the focus of this work.

D. Spiritual Growth Entails Bringing the Lower Chakras into Alignment with the Higher

Principle #2 on energy dynamics notes that the higher levels inform and integrate the lower, and Figure 4 provides an image of the higher chakras in relation to the lower. One traditional understanding of the soul spoke of the higher and a lower part, and that makes sense in the light of our present topic. If we were to draw a horizontal line through Figure 4 at the level of the 4th chakra, we would have two such divisions — a lower where psychological and biological issues prevail, and a higher, where thought has greater influence over the psyche and the body. This roughly corresponds with St. John of the Cross's teaching on a Dark Night of the Senses, which is concerned with healing the psyche, and a Night of the Spirit, which deals with thoughts and attitudes — the higher chakras. For St. John, the Dark Nights were necessary so the soul could come under greater influence of divine grace, mediated through the mind.

Bringing the lower chakras into alignment with the higher is a basic developmental challenge. We have little impulse control for the first few months of life, and only gradually learn to use our minds to express our emotions in socially appropriate ways. Further developing the power of the intellect to think and understand, and the will to discern and choose wisely can take a lifetime. The likelihood of this happening is enhanced if the energies of bios and psuche are not working against our spiritual potential, but here we must say, again, that we are all wounded, to some degree, even those who seem to have it all together. Some might look good and rational on the outside, but most people have inner desires and feelings they wrestle with on a daily basis. Even the great St. Paul complained of a "thorn in the flesh" he wanted God to take away from him.[41] He also spoke of two movements in our nature — one that was attracted to the higher realms of faith, goodness and love, and another that was sinful and self-serving.[42] Growth unto the higher realms is countered within by a contrary movement against which we must strain, or else it will have its way with us and keep us in negativity. It is as though our human nature is something of a wild horse that must come under the guidance of its rational master, the human spirit, but it is not easily tamed.

Nevertheless, it is the human spirit and its capacity for thought that must provide the proper form and direction for one's life. This is accomplished through our own reflection on experience, our dialogue with others, through studying traditions of wisdom and guidance such as the great world religions provide. In the end, we must decide for ourselves: what do we believe? why? what thoughts will we encourage and live by? what is our philosophy of life? our values? It is the work of the 6th and 7th chakras to respond to these questions. If we fail to do so, we are stuck with the programming we've absorbed from our families and culture, which might not be entirely bad, but is second-hand.

We must also seek the assistance of a Power greater than ourselves to tame our unruly passions. Energy follows attention, but thought gives form to energy, and it takes powerful thoughts aided by divine grace to re-form and trans-form us. Philosophers and self-help gurus can point out helpful directions, but it's been my experience that the human mind, left to itself, is mostly powerless to effect lasting changes. The liberating virtues for chakras 4 - 6 listed in Table 4 describe some of the work we

---

[41] See 2 Cor. 12:7

[42] Romans 7

must do ourselves. We must strive to be loving, generous, honest, open and humble, etc., but it is the abandonment and surrender of chakra 7 that opens us to the power of God. This is the highest ideal: that all of the chakras come under the guidance of the divine, whose grace will bring forth healing, and order all of our energies and potentialities as they were meant to be.

6.

Kundalini Activation

Lot went to Joseph and said, 'Abba, as far as I can, I keep a moderate rule, with a little fasting, and prayer, and meditation, and quiet: and as far as I can I try to cleanse my heart of evil thoughts. What else should I do?' Then the hermit stood up and spread out his hands to heaven, and his fingers shone like ten flames of fire, and he said, "If you will, you can become all flame."

This story from the desert fathers is a good introduction to the topic of kundalini activation.

What we have called the kundalini dynamic thus far moves slowly but surely from lower to higher consciousness, ever-prodding one to wake up and grow. It seems that resolving issues of biological survival alone are insufficient to satisfy our human longings, as the soul also seeks to become fully alive in its embodied state. This yearning is evidenced in the natural human tendency to more deeply explore our world, ourselves, questions of meaning, and relationships of love. The chakra system provides a language for describing how a soul gradually wakes up . . . or goes to sleep. The kundalini dynamic can be frustrated, with consequences to our mental, psychological and physical health. And yet it is this very dynamic that continually pushes against our maladaptations, prompting us to change, to seek assistance, to shed our chains and become free. In times past, this would have been called a "natural grace," which is to say that it is a gift inscribed in our human nature that can lead us to the supernatural grace that only God can provide.

People who faithfully respond to the inner "push" of the kundalini dynamic will find ways to grow. They will discover God's own Holy Spirit ever ready to lead them to others, books, groups circumstances, etc. that will help them to become healed and to learn the lessons they need. Even if they have never heard of the Holy Spirit,[43] that does not seem to matter, for God is good and gracious and ever-ready to assist anyone who is a sincere seeker of love, truth and wisdom. Another way of saying this is that those who attempt to live by the liberating virtues associated with the various chakras will find divine assistance coming to their aid. This, I believe, is the meaning of the Catholic teaching that people from any religion can be saved through fidelity to conscience.[44] On the other hand, even those who claim to know Jesus Christ and are active in his Church will grieve the Spirit if they do not live by these virtues.[45]

Fidelity to the kundalini dynamic is most commonly manifest in people who live an "ordinary" life. They might be religious, but not necessarily so. Most are hampered to some extent by woundings of the lower chakras, with unresolved psychological issues skewing their understanding of themselves and others. They have begun to awaken in the higher chakras, but have not yet done the hard work at the level of thought to clarify for themselves the deeper questions of life. Thus are they capable of being manipulated by the lies and logical fallacies perpetuated by politicians and the marketplace. Their identity is rooted in self-image, which is enmeshed with familial and cultural expectations, but they also know that, at a deeper level, they are "more" than this. They have various addictions to keep

---

[43] Acts 19:2

[44] "Those who, through no fault of their own, do not know the Gospel of Christ or his Church, but who nevertheless seek God with a sincere heart, and, moved by grace, try in their actions to do his will as they know it through the dictates of their conscience - those too may achieve eternal salvation."
Vatican II: *Lumen Gentium.* 16.

[45] Ephesians 4:30

them going, and hesitate to give them up out of fear. God is important to them, and provides a basis of meaning for their lives, but they do not have a living relationship with God and are not quite sure how to go about developing one. They probably watch too much TV, drink too much alcohol, eat too much junk food, etc., but . . . they are basically good-hearted people! When push comes to shove, they will help out another in need, and if God comes knocking, inviting a deeper relationship, they will usually respond.

Ignition

Kundalini activation marks an intensification of the kundalini dynamic, as tension exerted in spiritual consciousness stirs the lower levels to a greater supportive role. Another way to put this is that as the attentional motives of the higher chakras become more developed, this will necessitate a new ordering of energies in the soul.

Why does this happen?

There are many precipitating factors, some of them related to stress and trauma. In my own case, kundalini activation was associated with financial stress and doing group therapy for hours every day at a psychiatric hospital, where I was exposed to intense negative energy. My primary way of coping was to spend long periods in quiet prayer, allowing the energy to move out of my system through tears and coughing, leaving me feeling whole and peaceful and ready for another day.[46] But this also brought about a deepening of my prayer to realms beyond thought and imagery, and into the "zone" of the dynamic Ground

---

[46] See Chapter 1 in *Kundalini Energy and Christian Spirituality: A Pathway to Growth and Healing* (New York, NY: Crossroads, Publ., 1991.)

of consciousness, or the Apex of the soul. There, I found quiet, and I enjoyed resting in this zone for long periods of time — hours in some cases. This changed the alignment of energies within, as my pneuma became more rooted and stimulated by the vibration of the Ground.

My own experience is by no means definitive or normative, of course, but I have noted that it shares one characteristic with many other accounts of kundalini activation, namely: *apophatic experience.* By this, I am referring to a manner of prayer and meditation that goes beyond words and symbols of any kind — an opening to deep, non-conceptual silence. Apophatic spirituality is contrasted with *kataphatic spirituality*, which makes use of words, concepts, symbols, images, etc. in one's approach to God. I have always made use of this pathway, too, and consider it essential to the proper formation of thought and, hence, consciousness. It is also a means of contact with God, who is willing to communicate to us through the medium of created forms. Of course, not everyone who practices apophatic spirituality evidences kundalini activation, but almost everyone who has active kundalini has been involved with apophatic practice. The correlation is very strong!

Examples of apophatic disciplines include centering prayer, zen meditation, TM, vipassana, breathing prayer, the Jesus Prayer, Christian Meditation, and speaking in tongues. Most of the accounts of kundalini activation and awakening included in Appendix 2 involved at least one of these practices. The idea in all of them is to reduce or frustrate mental activity so that one eventually comes to experience a deeper state of awareness — non-reflecting awareness, which has always been there, but is usually clouded with thoughts, images, feelings, etc. Ideally, it is contemplative grace that draws one to this deeper rest, but this need not be the case. Not all experiences of non-conceptual awareness are mystical, though all are at least experiences of the human spirit in its non-reflecting aspect. They are also, to some degree, experiences of closer proximity to the Apex, where we receive our existence from God moment-by-moment. It may be that the kundalini dynamic is the push that moves us there, or the pull of divine grace, or, most likely, both.

Everything mentioned above is about what is happening at the level of attention, which raises the question of what is going on with us energetically during apophatic practice? What happens to our energies when we spend more and more time in deep silence? Without the formative influence of thought, where does energy go, and what does it do?

In many cases, it seems that energy continues to flow within along the patterns established by our usual habits of mind and will. These, in turn, are the fruit of regular spiritual practice. So, in most cases, all is well, and when/if the energy seems to begin to become disruptive, then it's easy enough to back off on time spent in apophatic meditation and resume normal activities. In such cases, we can speak of an intensified and integrated kundalini dynamic, or even an integrated activation.

The more difficult cases of activation seem to happen if:

a. One is a relative newcomer to the spiritual life and begins to use apophatic methods for extended periods of time.

b. One suddenly intensifies the use of apophatic methods, as during a retreat, or Lent, or during a period of stress.

c. One receives shaktipat (energy touch) from someone with heightened kundalini before being properly prepared. This possibility includes being prayed over by an individual or group, as in a charismatic prayer meeting.[47]

d. No good reason; it just seems to happen spontaneously.

The most difficult cases are those from examples a and d, as the activation happens without the recipient having established a proper foundation for energy integration. A challenge for them is to find a way to to this in the midst of energy struggles that can leave them confused, depressed and discouraged.

With kundalini activation, it seems that some kind of inner "switch" is tripped, signaling a new relationship between the Ground and the levels of consciousness. In most cases, the change happens as a consequence of extended periods of apophatic practice, where attention is directed "upward" to the higher chakras and beyond, to non-conceptual consciousness and the divine. Doing this for extended periods, day after day, one's integrative center of attention, the Ego,[48] is raised higher and higher, with energy dynamics shifting accordingly. Increasing tension is introduced into the soul, as the pneuma becomes increasingly rooted in the Apex, which in turn increases the vibrational intensity of pneuma.[49] A new "normal" of internal energy dynamics becomes established. It's as though the voltage

---

[47] One way to understand shaktipat is that it is like jump-starting a car with a weakened battery. The current from stronger battery moves through jumper cables to add power to the weaker. In many cases, this is the "spark" that triggers kundalini activation.

[48] This use of the term, Ego, is not meant to be disparaging, but is congruent with the use in Jung's psychology. See also *God and I: Exploring the Connections Between God, Self and Ego*, by Philip St. Romain (Raleigh, NC: Lulu Press, 2016)

[49] I do not especially like using the language of "vibration," as I have no scientific basis for doing so. Even though books have been written about chakra vibrations and vibrational medicine, I think it's best to consider this kind of language to be metaphorical.

of the human energy system is being raised from 110 to 220, with consequences similar to what we observe when we do this with electrical wiring: eventually, things will "heat up," with pneumatic vibration resounding through the levels of psyche and organism as well. For awhile, one feels more alive and healthy than ever, but that is usually difficult to sustain without making serious lifestyle changes. In more intense activations and awakenings, the whole system can eventually become acutely stressed, as the intensified pneuma "burns up" one's reserves of psuche and bios, leaving one feeling empty and exhausted. Becoming "all flame" is a lofty ideal, but it takes considerable fuel to keep the fire burning.

This is as good a place as any to note that not all activations are permanent. Some episodes might be better called *kundalini arousals*, as they are brief in duration, as during a retreat, for example, or a stressful time in life. In such cases, the energy phenomena die down when one cuts back on spiritual practice for awhile. Nevertheless, the inner activation switch alluded to above has been loosened, and it is common to find activations recurring when spiritual practice is again intensified.

One common question I've heard many times through the years is "how do you turn it off?" This inquiry is especially urgent from those who were not well-prepared for kundalini activation, but somehow triggered it inadvertently through a period of intense apophatic practice, for example. They would gladly go back to the way things were before, problems and all, but do not know how to do so. Besides cutting back on or giving up spiritual practice for awhile, and introducing more red meat and grounding exercises into their lives, there is not much else one can do. Any time they sit quietly for just a few moments, the process revs up again, and can be even more disquieting precisely because they have cut back on spiritual disciplines.

Sometimes, things do fade out in time, but usually one will need to learn how to live with the activation, like it or not. Such cases have convinced me beyond any doubt that we are dealing, here, with a phenomenon that is distinct from Holy Spirit blessing.

Consequences of Activation

What happens when the intensity of the human energy system is elevated, or when we raise the energy thermostat within, to use a different metaphor?

The three levels of human nature — organism, psyche and spirit — and their respective energies of bios, psuche and pneuma will become more stimulated as well.

Sometimes, this is experienced as inner heat, or perhaps bubbling sensations of energy, or even zings of electrical flow. The bizarre sensations that accompany an activation are many, and they can change all through the day. One can feel a tightness in one place, warm flow of energy in another, inner lights, sounds, and other phenomena listed in Chapter 1. These are concomitant to the activation, which in turn is often concomitant to deepening union with God. Let's examine more closely the changes happening in our human nature.

Spirit-level: intensified pneuma

- Often, the awakening of psychic gifts like intuitive knowing, clairvoyance and healing.

- Inductive reasoning comes easily, though deductive logic is still accessible and sometimes used in daily living.

- Heightened sensitivity to the consequences of thoughts. Constricting thoughts become easily distinguished from open, loving thoughts. Less judgmentalism.

- Right and left brain processes are more stimulated and integrated. Sometimes the whole brain feels warm and tingly, filled with life and power.

- A new center of awareness becomes established in the center of the forehead — the 3rd eye — enabling a kind of "single-seeing" attuned to the present moment. In this state, one is immediately aware of inner and outer phenomena, but drawn to that which needs attention.

- Capacity for inner silence. The mind is mostly quiet.

- Some kind of "antenna" is attuned to guidance from above and embodiment below.

- One feels whole, connected, open to the outer and inner world.

- Acute sensitivity to relationship between attention and energy — how one can "push" or move energy within oneself using attention.

- There are astonishing cases where kundalini activation was accompanied by knowledge of other languages, proficiency doing math, composing music, writing poetry, or other skills one had only minimal proficiency at before. Gopi Krishna, for example, wrote several books in poetic verse form, allowing the words to simply flow, he said.

- Overall creativity is enhanced, including relational intelligence.

Psyche level: intensified psuche

- Repressed emotional energies flushed out from body's tissues. Often, one does not even have the memory of what the incidents were about. Tears, sighs and breath evacuating the energy.

- Loss of affective memory. One can remember events, but the feelings once associated with them are gone.

- Archetypal energies of unconscious stirred. Dreams and inner images of snakes, angels, devils, mythical creatures appear, at times.[50]

- Heightened empathy to others. Compassion.

- Loosening hold of self-image on identity. One comes to see how the memory creates self-image, but that one's true identity is more than this.

- Depression and emptiness during times of depletion.

Organism level: intensified bios

- Inadvertent jerks and movements of the body to facilitate energy flow, these often coming during sleep. Many of these movements are similar to yogic asanas.

- Occasional sleep disturbances.

- Sensations of energy bubbling and fizzing through the body.

- Distinct sense of energy being blocked in places, and of "pushing" with attention to move the energy through. Sometimes, blocked energy causing headaches and pain in other parts of the body.

---

[50] Perhaps kundalini activation is associated with some of the phenomena reported in the Toronto Blessing, a Christian pentecostal group meeting at the Toronto Airport Vineyard Church for over 20 years. In addition to the usual charismatic gifts of speaking in tongues, prophecy, deepening faith and healings, some participants were slain in the Spirit, falling to the ground in apparent unconsciousness for brief periods. Others evidenced jerking movements in their bodies, as with kundalini kryas; still others made strange animal noises, like pigs, or lions or hyenas. What is suggested is kundalini activation accompanying a deepening surrender to the Holy Spirit, with the archetypes of the unconscious manifesting in certain cases.
- see https://en.wikipedia.org/wiki/Toronto_Blessing#Negative_Impact

- Hyper-stimulation of sexual feelings, usually a brief phase.

- Changes in appetite. Aversion to certain foods that are presumably in conflict with maintaining bios. Times of intense hunger.

- Sense of reproductive fluids being taken up into the process. Feelings of depletion and rawness when sexual fluids are excessively depleted.

- Feeling of energy stimulating a place deep in the brain, sometimes with intensity, in the center of the forehead.

- More sensitivity of the five senses, especially the senses of smell and hearing.

- Change in breathing patterns at times. Spontaneous pranayama. Shallow, empty breath when bios is diminished.

- Acute exhaustion during times of bios depletion.

Not all of these changes happen at once, and many do not occur at all in some individuals. But most people with kundalini activation can easily check off most of them after a few months. Small wonder we are given strange looks when we try to share what's happening to us with others who do not know about kundalini. Even doctors and counselors are often at a loss as to what to say or recommend. This contributes to a sense of loneliness and isolation, as the activation process is not common even among those engaged in contemplative practice. Thankfully, the Internet has made it possible for "kundalini people" to find each other and to at least affirm that we are still "on the map," as it were, of human experience.

Obviously, many of the changes listed above are very positive, but others are quite a struggle. My sense is that the point of it all is the transformations taking place at the level of the human spirit, which is now becoming increasingly open to its

Apex or inner connection with the divine. But spiritual transformation must be accompanied by supportive changes in the psyche and organism levels so that this new higher spiritual consciousness can be embodied and sustained. That's what kundalini activation is about, in a nutshell.

Lifestyle Changes

Although this book is meant to be more descriptive and reflective than pastoral, a few comments on lifestyle adjustments are in order, here. During the early days of kundalini activation, many have a difficult time carrying on with business as usual. Work that requires mental focus and intellectual analysis will be especially stressful, as will casual conversations. Sometimes, fluorescent lighting is annoying; background music as is found in some workplaces can seem distasteful. Junk food doesn't sit well, alcohol might cause severe mood swings, and TV is bothersome. Even if one had been diligent about living a healthy lifestyle before the activation, there will be stressors. Often times, one cannot even read much, not even books on spirituality. Any kind of mental concentration stirs things up within, often uncomfortably so.

The cause of these difficulties is largely related to the intensified pneuma and the extraordinary demands this places on the psyche and organism, at least for awhile. Intensified pneuma is extremely sensitive to mental stimulation within oneself and from others. This is not all bad, as it helps one become more aware of the formative power of thoughts that we might become more responsible at this level. Energy follows attention, and thought forms attention, so the integration of energy and attention entails hard work at the level of thought, and this is not easy when one is being bombarded by a wide range of thoughts from various sources.

I've often thought of early kundalini activation as a situation similar to that which crustaceans face during their life cycle. Animals like crabs and crawfish have an exoskeleton, which they need to shed several times during their lives to accommodate their growing bodies. During the interim between shedding the old shell and growing a new one, they are very vulnerable, and usually hide out to avoid prey. Eventually, when their new shell hardens a bit, they can resume normal life. Something like this is a good idea during early activation as well, if one can do so. A lifestyle that is quiet, simple, with few stressors and demands is ideal. Often, as was my situation, this is impossible, so one carries on as well as possible.

In time, the process itself is our best teacher. We learn what foods are helpful, and which are not; how much time to spend in prayer or meditation; how much TV we can watch; what are the signals when we are approaching excessive reading, and so forth. But in almost every case I have ever come across, the general tendency is to live a simpler, quieter lifestyle, with more time for spiritual practice, walks in nature, and the pursuit of enjoyable hobbies. A healthy diet, exercise, and good sleep are also necessary; some web sites provide extensive information on herbs and other supplements that help. A few people have told me they cannot stand to be in a city beyond a few days before becoming depleted of energy — perhaps the pollution, noise, or some other subtle factors.

Travel to visit family and friends can be an ordeal, as one is taken out of one's stabilizing lifestyle and plunged into another environment where, generally, people do not pray, and where there is going-and-doing from morning until night, often with the TV on, music in the background, idle chatter, and so forth. Some adjust by trying to carve out their own space in the guest room where they stay, or by renting a hotel room. I have often used the excuse of needing time and space to avoid a migraine, and others accept it (it is the truth). It is not easy, for relationships with family and friends are important and require personal investments of time and energy — even sacrifices.

All of which is to say that there were very good reasons why kundalini process was something of an occult science in Hinduism for many centuries. This was not something for ordinary people to pursue; the ashram or monastery provided an ideal setting for developing a foundation and supporting integration. It is also why, in Christianity, apophatic practices were not encouraged for ordinary lay people such as they are today. It was recognized that all sorts of fireworks could arise as a consequence of this kind of spirituality, and that a monastery or religious community could help to deal with this. Alas, now there are a plethora of books on apophatic spirituality, and many people take them up without first establishing a proper inner foundation through kataphatic prayer, study, and the pursuit of virtue. These are the hardest kundalini cases to deal with, but they are not beyond God's power to resolve. What needs to be emphasized most strongly is that anyone undertaking apophatic spiritual practices ought to be under the guidance of a spiritual director to help discern what's going on, when to back off, when God is calling one to go deeper, and so forth. It would also be great if spiritual directors knew more about kundalini activation, but that is not always the case. Hopefully, this book will provide a helpful resource to them.

7.

Kundalini and Christianity

There is no instance of the use of the term "kundalini" the the Bible or Christian teaching, but neither is there mention of the psychological unconscious, complexes, neuroses, peak experiences, Dark Nights of the Soul, spiritual aridity— many kinds of psycho-spiritual and physiological phenomena. That is because the central focus of the Christian religion is theological — how God, through Jesus Christ, has brought healing and Spirit-blessing to the human race through the life, death and resurrection of Jesus. Through faith and Baptism, a Christian connects to this new life, or *Zoe*, and becomes a member of a Christian community, where the Spirit gifts us to ministry. This is the primary interest of the New Testament. Moral and spiritual practices are also taught, but they are not considered in themselves to be the means of salvation or connection with God so much as how one co-operates with the transformative power of the Spirit, Who is pure gift, or grace.

It is a commonly held belief among all Christians that the period of Divine Revelation ended with the death of the last Apostle around 100 A.D. Nevertheless, our understanding of how God works in human nature has continued to grow through the centuries. In recent decades, this understanding has become enriched through dialogue between Christians and members of other religions, who have developed their own spiritual traditions. That is why we are now, in this work, examining possible resonances between kundalini process and Christian teaching and experience.

Kundalini in the Bible?

For Christians, the legitimacy and value of a spiritual/ religious belief or practice is usually discerned in the light of Scripture. Minimally, it must not go *against* what Scripture teaches; ideally, it is explicitly *sanctioned* in Scripture. My sense is that the kind of teaching I have presented in this book belongs to the former judgment rather than the latter. This is not a huge problem for Catholics like myself, however, as we have long adopted the attitude expressed by Paul in Rm. 14:19, "Let us adopt any custom that leads to peace and our mutual improvement." There is also Jesus' attitude, "whoever is not against us is for us" (Lk. 9:50). Thus have Catholics made use of teachings and practices from various cultures and philosophies in the service of the Gospel. Indeed, the teaching on the soul presented in this book is largely informed by St. Thomas Aquinas, who was deeply influenced by the Greek philosopher, Aristotle.

There are a few places in Scripture that hint of kundalini, however. One is Rom. 8:22, where Paul writes of the "whole creation groaning in one great act of giving birth." This suggests an evolutionary dynamic that we humans, too, who are part of the creation, experience as well. For Paul, it is the gift of the Spirit that fulfills this longing and brings satisfaction, but the developmental impetus seems intrinsic to creation itself. This resonates with the understanding of the kundalini dynamic presented in the book as an inner entelechy[51] that "pushes" the creature from within unto its unfolding while the Spirit gently pulls and guides us.

---

[51] *Entelechy* refers to an inner drive aiming at the fulfillment of a creature's potential. E.g., it is entelechy for the acorn to become an oak tree, or a child to become an adult human person.

There is also 1 Tim. 1:6, where Paul tells Timothy "to fan into flame the gift of God, which is in you through the laying on of my hands." The laying on of hands — quite common in early Christianity — can be understood as a kind of Christian shaktipat which, in this case, apparently stirred things up in the young disciple, Timothy, when Paul prayed over him. This sounds like it could be an instance where kundalini activation and Holy Spirit blessing come together, as we will explore more deeply in a section below.

In 1 Cor. 14, Paul expresses concern about the lack of order in the Church of Corinth. It seems that people there are really whooping it up in the Spirit, perhaps in a manner similar to the Toronto Blessing, which was mentioned in our previous chapter. Paul calls for order and reason to prevail.

Then there's the strange reference by John the Baptist in Mt. 3:11 to Jesus baptizing in "the Holy Spirit and fire." It could be that "fire" is reinforcing the meaning of "Spirit," as it is one of the symbols of the Spirit. But still I wonder, especially with Jesus' saying in Mark 9:49 that "everyone will be salted with fire." Biblical scholars puzzle over this, most noting that it probably refers to a purification process. That is certainly what kundalini activation accomplishes in us.

I hesitate to link kundalini with the story of the temptation of Adam and Eve in the Garden of Eden by the serpent, as there are so many mythological themes in play. But the bait held out by the devil — "when you eat it, your eyes will be opened, and you will be like God, knowing good and evil"[52] — is suggestive of the higher spiritual consciousness that kundalini awakens. In punishment for this transgression of taking the fruit before its proper time, the couple are thrown out of the Garden, and the

---

[52] Genesis 3:5.

snake, too, is punished. Henceforth, it will crawl on its belly and eat dust,[53] which is a fitting way to speak of fallen, inactive kundalini. Granted that this is an interpretive stretch, but perhaps it highlights another angle of that multi-faceted story.

The story of the Tower of Babel story is another that resonates with the Fall.[54] Here we find people cooperating to build a tower that will reach to the heavens. God, in response, mixes up their languages and scatters them across the earth. The story is a continuing account of how the human race became estranged from God and one another, but the sin, in this case, is the effort to force our way into heaven using our own efforts. People who, without reference to God, attempt to use ascetical methods to empower the higher chakras and awaken kundalini are doing something similar. Heaven is God's realm, and we must be invited into it by God rather than trying to barge in on our own. As the stories of The Fall and Babel illustrate, we pay heavy consequences for doing so.

The story of the encounter between the Hebrew people and seraph (fiery) serpents in the desert is also worth mentioning.[55] Some scholars understand these serpents to be literal reptiles whose bites were tormenting the people; others take them in a more metaphorical sense as interior burning from a spiritual purgation that was taking place on the desert journey. Most interestingly, the fiery serpents bite them because they are complaining against God and Moses, which would introduce negativity and blockages into their system. Moses is instructed to "make a fiery serpent of bronze and put it on a pole, and

---

[53] Genesis 3:15.

[54] Genesis 11:1-9.

[55] Numbers 21:4-9.

everyone who is bitten will live when he looks at it." Moses did so, and people who'd been bitten were healed when they looked upon this symbol. We don't know what that rod and serpent looked like, but it is strongly suggestive of a Caduceus (which had two snakes) or a Rod of Asclepius, both of which are ancient symbols of divine power.

What is most intriguing about the seraph serpent story and the serpent on the rod is that Jesus relates this to his own crucifixion: "Just as Moses lifted up the snake in the wilderness, even so must the Son of Man be lifted up; that everyone who believes may have eternal life in him."[56] The language of *lifting up the serpent* certainly resonates with kundalini process, and it is even more curious that Jesus identifies himself in some manner with that bronze serpent. Even if biblical scholarship cannot affirm a kundalini meaning to these passages, one can still take away from them the point that on our own, we cannot deal with the power of kundalini once it is activated within us. We need Christ to set things right within and among us.

Kundalini and the Demonic

A few years ago, I received a phone call from a cousin who wanted to know why I'd written a book on kundalini. He'd heard a preacher on the radio denouncing kundalini yoga as a demonic practice, and so he was concerned for my soul and what I was into. In going through old email exchanges while planning this book, I found similar questions asked. One man recently went so far as to tell me that two priests with vast experience in exorcisms had assured him that kundalini was of the devil, and he should read nothing about this nor have anything to do with me or anyone else who might disagree with them.

---

[56] John 3:14-15.

Obviously, there are many Christian leaders who react negatively to teachings about kundalini. Most likely, they are superficially familiar with the yogic teaching about kundalini being Shakti, a goddess, whose energy moves up the spine to unite with Shiva, the Hindu god of awareness and power. They also know that kundalini is sometimes called the "serpent power," as dreams of serpents are common during kundalini awakenings and activations. To them, this all smacks of idolatry, and they believe the reference to serpents to be a clear allusion to the devil, who appeared to Adam and Even in serpentine form in the Garden of Eden.

I can't say I blame Christian leaders for their concern, as the Shakti, Shiva, serpent symbolism is a stretch for any Christian theology to accommodate. But what we have in the Hindu accounting is just one way of thematizing what is a universal phenomenon. Ignoring the Hindu symbolism, for the moment, one can inquire whether the symptoms of kundalini process described in Chapter 1, the powers of the chakras described in Chapter 5, and the activation process discussed in Chapter 6 can be observed outside of Hinduism, and the answer is clearly yes. Wherever apophatic spirituality is practiced and emphasized, one can expect to find kundalini activations and awakenings, and that is indeed the case. Space does not permit a detailed listing and description of kundalini at work in other religions and spiritualities; some of the stories shared in Appendix 2 allude to this. The problem for us is that there is not one universal term to apply to this phenomenon, but the one that seems to be used most frequently across a wide spectrum of disciplines is "kundalini." Obviously, when Buddhists use the term, they are not referencing Shakti and Shiva; neither are Taoists, or Zen practitioners.

The relation between kundalini and the demonic needs to be clarified, here, especially since that is the usual concern among well-meaning Christian leaders. How could one tell if the symptoms manifesting were from God, the devil, or the unconscious? Of course, even to frame the question this way is different from the approach taken by many ministers, who do not factor in the unconscious in their considerations. In their anthropology, the only actors on the stage of the individual's life are God, the Ego, and the devil. When analyzing a phenomenon like kundalini, it doesn't take long to rule out God or the Ego as the cause, so that leaves only the devil to blame. Obviously, this approach is too short-sighted!

Beginning in the early 20th C. and proceeding to this day, modern psychology has explored this inner realm that we call the unconscious. It encompasses the levels of organism, psyche and spirit, and is the source for a wide range of desires, energies and symbols. Many ministers eschew modern psychology, however, and that is a problem. Nevertheless, it is true that demonic influence can work through the unconscious, although it would seem to require a considerable amount of time and psychiatric evaluation to make this determination. Roman Catholic exorcism doesn't even begin to proceed until mental health issues have been ruled out, and thus there have been very few in the U.S. since that approach was adopted. There are cases that psychology cannot fully account for, however, and which might signal the presence of a demon. A few tell-tale signs:[57]

- Loss or lack of appetite

- Cutting, scratching, and biting of skin

---

[57] Wikipedia entry on exorcism in the Catholic Church
https://en.wikipedia.org/wiki/
Exorcism_in_the_Catholic_Church#When_an_exorcism_is_needed

- A cold feeling in the room

- Unnatural bodily postures and change in the person's face and body

- The possessed losing control of their normal personality and entering into a frenzy or rage, and/or attacking others

- Change in the person's voice

- Supernatural physical strength not subject to the person's build or age

- Speaking or understanding another language which they had never learned before

- Knowledge of things that are distant or hidden

- Prediction of future events (sometimes through dreams)

- Levitation and moving of objects / things

- Expelling of objects / things

- Intense hatred and violent reaction toward all religious objects or items

- Antipathy towards entering a church, speaking Jesus' name or hearing scripture.

One problem is that some of these signs are often associated with pentecostalism and mystical experiences, including levitation, prophetic visions and knowledge, and speaking other languages. Even the negative, self-destructive, anti-religious symptoms cannot be considered sure signs of possession, but could be related to some kind of anti-social disorder. In other words, labeling someone as possessed or under the influence of the devil is tricky business.

Hopefully, one contribution of this book and others on the topic would be to recognize that *the kundalini process is, in and of itself, a natural phenomenon that is morally and spiritually neutral.* Kundalini can work in synchrony with the God's grace to bring about great good in an individual, but it could also be activated in a context of evil as well, as in a cult, for example, or idolatry, or demon worship. In such cases, the pneuma, psuche and bios would be more stimulated, with similar signs and symptoms as in a healthy activation, but the accompanying moral behavior and spiritual fruits would be very different. Also, I suspect, kundalini in the service of evil could not produce the high degree of inner healing and integration that one finds when it is working in synchrony with the Holy Spirit. It could also be enmeshed with the kundalini of others, producing a bondage situation. In short, it could make a dark experience darker, but the fault here is not kundalini so much as the quality of attention it is augmenting.

The energy enmeshment issue is especially significant with regard to shaktipat, which has been mentioned several times in this work. One woman I know could not shake off a sense that the guru who'd given her shaktipat was still somehow influencing her energies years after the experience! The guru was not an unpleasant presence, just an un-welcomed one. By the time we met, she'd become a Christian and wanted nothing more to do with him, but she couldn't seem to extinguish the energy bond established with him from years later.

Sometimes the bond is not pleasant, but is quite negative, as Anon5 shared in Appendix 2. I got to know him well. The psychic healers he mentions in his story continued to influence him in mysterious ways years after the experience, often tormenting him during sleep. Another person I came to know received shaktipat from a Siddha Yoga guru and felt like his consciousness was negatively influenced by the guru. Shaktipat apparently establishes a deep energy bond between the guru and the disciple — a dynamic that is actually sought out in some yogic circles as a help unto growth. But problems arise when/if one wishes to break this bond, or when the guru's energy is contaminated by vices.

I recall years ago, after delivering a lecture at a kundalini conference, being approached by a man of about 40 who introduced himself to me as an "energy therapist," and said there were imbalances in my auric field he could correct if I let him "work on me." The hair on my back stood up when I heard this, and I politely declined, but he continued to impose this suggestion several more times before finally going away. My general policy is to not allow anyone to do any kind of "energy work" with me unless it's in the context of Christian ministry.

There are risks with shaktipat and various forms of subtle energy work, but there's no doubt that many, many people receive benefit from these as well. Nevertheless, one should be cautious and discerning in seeking these interventions.[58]

Pentecostal Phenomena

What we now call pentecostal spirituality was apparently common in the early Church, where we read of people speaking in tongues, prophesying, working miracles, healing, and so forth. In time, those phenomena seem to have subsided, prompting many to suggest that they were necessary for early believers, but that once liturgical, educational, institutional and theological traditions became established, they were no longer necessary. But beginning in the early 20th C. with a small group of

---

[58] U.S. Catholic Bishops have published a number of concerns in a document entitled "Guidelines for Evaluating Reiki as an Alternative Therapy." 2009.
http://www.usccb.org/_cs_upload/8092_1.pdf

Christians, modern pentecostalism eventually developed into a significant movement in Christianity, spreading to many denominations while developing their own denominations as well. In the mainline Protestant churches and Roman Catholicism, it became called the Charismatic Movement, with prayer groups meeting regularly in parishes, especially from the late 1960s through the early 80s. There are a few such groups today, but pentecostalism seems to be thriving more in non-denominational Christian communities and in denominations like United Pentecostal Churches International and World Assemblies of God fellowship. It is estimated that there are over 279 million pentecostals worldwide.

A primary emphasis in modern pentecostalism is the baptism of the Spirit, which is usually administered to believers through the laying on of hands after a preparatory period of study and prayer. The chief sign that one has received this baptism is that the recipient begins to speak in tongues — a charismatic gift called *glossolalia*.[59] In some cases, this utterance is of a real foreign language that is understood by someone close by, but in most cases it is a murmuring of incoherent syllables that make no sense to anyone. Generally, it is a gift to enhance one's personal prayer connection with God, as the Apostle Paul notes:

> For anyone who speaks in a tongue does not speak to people but to God. Indeed, no one understands them; they utter mysteries by the Spirit. But the one who prophesies speaks to people for their strengthening, encouraging and comfort. Anyone who speaks in a tongue edifies themselves, but the one who prophesies edifies the church.[60]

---

[59] Not everyone who is prayed for receives the gift of tongues, but in many communities, it is regarded as the definitive sign of Spirit baptism.

[60] 1 Cor. 14:2-4.

In public worship, Paul would like the gift of tongues to be used with discretion, as a catalyst for prophetic messages. But he clearly acknowledges the personal nature of the prayer as well.

I received this gift when two dear friends prayed for me to receive the baptism of the Spirit in the fall of 1973, and it has been an important part of my prayer life since. It arises during my prayer times and even throughout the day, especially when I am driving around. Those who do not have this gift find it incomprehensible, and I once thought the same as well. But it seems connected with breathing — that the tongue is moved to prayerfully express certain syllables during the breathing process. One can surely choose not to give utterance aloud or even under one's breath; it is not a case of possession of any kind. It is also possible to consciously choose to pray this way, and often the gift aspect emerges shortly thereafter. Generally, the experience is short-lived, maybe a few minutes at most. Always, it seems, there is a deepening sense of peace and connection with God that comes from this form of prayer. Sometimes, deep insights follow as well, or a prophetic message from God. It's as though the prayer opens a channel for the Spirit to work in the soul. I consider it to be a type of mystical contemplation, as it is non-discursive, though not in the manner of many apophatic prayer forms. It is certainly a bridge to contemplative rest.

One thing I have noticed is that praying in tongues stimulates the kundalini process in people who have experienced activation. It most likely leads to activation as well, and I believe it played such a role in my own experience. The synchrony between sound syllables and breath creates an inner vibration that seems to both intensify and harmonize the energies of the soul. I've wondered about the depth from which tongues emerge, as it is far deeper than thought, and in light of the framework articulated in this book, I am inclined to say that it emerges from the Ground of Being under the influence of the Spirit. When it happens like that, any energies that are stirred up will also be balanced and harmonized. If, however, one pushes too hard and persists in speaking in tongues beyond the movement of grace, it could intensify energy in an unhealthy way — and, yes, this kind of willfulness is possible, though not common, I suspect.

There is a shaktipat dynamic at work in pentecostalism, as noted in other parts of this book. The laying on of hands to request Spirit baptism is somewhat like yogic shaktipat, but is also different in that those praying are asking God, or Christ, or the Spirit to move through them to bless another person. These pray-ers offer themselves as a channel through which God can work rather than as the source of the spark of energy transmitted.

Once the kundalini process is activated, it continues to do its work, and evidence of this can be seen in charismatics. All of the symptoms and movements described in Chapters 1 and 6 can be noted, at times, though the severity generally seems to be reduced. That is because the gift of tongues emerges when things get too stuck to help them flow along and balance out. Still, there can be difficult times for pentecostals, as anyone who continues to grow spiritually will be led to the Dark Nights of the Soul that St. John of the Cross discussed in his classical work.[61] In very extreme cases, where worship might go on an on, kundalini activation can become very discomfiting for awhile. There have been numerous accounts of this on my discussion forum, and I have experienced this as well.

The relationship between pentecostalism and kundalini requires more investigation than I can provide in this work. My

---

[61] St. John of the Cross. *Dark Night of the Soul*. (E. Allison Peers translation). (Garden City, NY: Doubleday/Image., 1959)

hunch is that most pentecostals would probably be resistant to understanding kundalini activation as part of what's going on in their experiences, but I also hope that they do not believe that they are somehow exempt from the dynamic of "grace acting upon nature," as St. Thomas Aquinas put it. Pentecostalism is likely the safest and most effective approach to awakening and integrating kundalini process in the Christian religion, especially if it is accompanied by theological/biblical studies and attention to psychological issues. I don't know where I'd be without the gift of tongues and dare not even speculate. Indeed, I can't imagine life without either of these gifts, and thank God for them. My hope is that others who struggle with kundalini integration will look into the Charismatic Movement to see how they might be blessed by it as well.

Theological Considerations

All throughout this work, we have considered the philosophical and theological implications of kundalini process. Chapter 2, for example, was an extensive reflection by Jim Arraj on this topic, so what I'd like to offer here are just a few remarks by way of summary.

1. There is a distinction between the kundalini process and the Holy Spirit. Although the two are often intertwined, it is also possible to recognize both in terms of origin and the fruits we see manifesting from them. Countless people around the world give evidence of the presence of the Spirit in their lives without any indication of kundalini activation. It is more difficult to find the opposite, but anyone with activated or awakened kundalini can attest to the difference. Kundalini goes on and on, often painfully so, with energy movements one can interact with and influence attentionally. It just "feels" like a natural process, and there's often a rawness or even violence about it. In time, however, we learn that it is part of who one is — not some foreign force that has invaded the soul, but energies of the soul that are being re-integrated.

The Holy Spirit has an entirely different feel about it — light, joyous, buoyant, loving, gifting one for service. Its blessings come and go as the Spirit pleases; it is not within our attentional control. We can open and dispose ourselves to being so gifted, but Spirit anointing can fall upon one at any time. When this happens in those with activated kundalini, things fall into place more easily. Kundalini might still be a struggle, but not so much of one. It might be a "thorn in the flesh," but one that we know God can use for our own good.

Theologically, then, kundalini, as a process rooted in the Ground of Being, belongs to the creation side of things while the Holy Spirit is divine. Writers from monistic traditions like Hinduism do not make this distinction, which is understandable. But Christianity is dualistic in the sense of recognizing a distinction between God and creation — that God makes creatures that are not-God and which possess their own measure of intelligence and freedom — consciously so, in the case of humans. Locating kundalini within the creation means that we ought to expect to find it manifesting at times in ways that seemingly have no religious perspective — that might even be anti-religious, or evil. This possibility was brought home above in our discussion about kundalini and the demonic. Also noteworthy is that this process can sometimes be triggered inadvertently, with no religious context whatsoever — as in lamaze breathing during childbirth or drug experiences.[62]

---

[62] See Christina and Stanislov Grof. *The Stormy Search for the Self.* (New York, NY: Jeremy P. Tarcher Ed., 1992)

The psycho-physiological conditions for triggering kundalini activation can happen in many ways that have nothing to do with religious spirituality. One woman who corresponded with me for years had an activation when she fell from a chair on her tailbone. We can't blame the devil or the Holy Spirit for that sort of thing. Gopi Krishna theorized that there could be a genetic basis for kundalini, and I suspect that accounts for some variation in the activation trigger. I've been unable to find any solid research to back up this hypothesis, so it will have to remain just that for now.

2. *The purpose of kundalini is to orient us to God.* This would include the low-intensity kundalini dynamic as well as activations and awakenings. Of course, this is also true about our intellect and will as well — they have an intrinsic orientation to ultimacy. But kundalini is a deeper, more persistent inner "push" to wake up and grow — a sacred unrest that constantly seeks to integrate all dimensions of our human nature in the Ground of our being, where we are naturally closest to God.

Like everything else about human nature, kundalini has become disordered because of sin — that dark, mysterious power at work in us that moves us away from God, one another, and the creation. Concretely, this is experienced as selfishness, narcissism and the four biases (dramatic, individual, social, general) described so brilliantly by Bernard Lonergan, S.J. and his explicators.[63] These biases either block or distort the flow of energy within, and support a false-self identity that we fabricate

---

[63] See pp. 67-68 in *Foundations of Spirituality: A Systematic Approach*, by Carla Mae Streeter (Collegeville, MN. Liturgical Press, 2012).

from a very early age.[64] But like a sapling trying to grow in rocky soil, kundalini exerts a constant resistance to these blocks, finally breaking through when it is intensified through spiritual practice or other factors. When it becomes fully activated, one becomes acutely aware of the embodied roots of biases and repressed emotions, which are loosened and evacuated, sometimes unpleasantly so. But the overall sense within is that "this is going somewhere, and it will be good," as the final goal of embodied higher spiritual consciousness is embedded in the process itself. This is why the full integration of kundalini implies a religious spirituality — some kind of conscious cooperation with God's grace. We need a "Higher Power" to properly direct this "lower power."

3. *Kundalini as concomitant experience.* Christianity has observed kundalini phenomena work in various mystics through the ages,[65] but has generally considered its characteristics concomitant phenomena, or an instance of *gratiae gratis data*.[66]

Saying that kundalini phenomena are concomitant to mystical experiences isn't saying much, however, as this doesn't really recognize the nature of the process or its purpose. It's merely noting that the phenomena accompany something else — mystical experiences, or spiritual transformation. Of course, if all that one is interested in is explicit mystical knowledge, then it would seem that kundalini has no significance whatsoever. I believe this is short-sighted, however, as the next point explains.

---

[64] Chapter 4 on "False Self System" in *God and I: Exploring the Connections Between God, Self and Ego* (Wichita, KS: Contemplative Ministries, Inc., 2016)

[65] The visions of inner light and other phenomena experienced by hesychasts comes to mind here.

[66] Special graces.

4. *Kundalini is vital to spiritual transformation.* This process is known as sanctification, deification, or theosis — how people of faith come to participate in the life of divinity. My spiritual director likens it to a paper towel being dipped into olive oil; it remains a paper towel, but is also saturated by the oil. Biblical images include fermentation processes like bread dough being baked into bread, and grape juice becoming wine. The initial substance is transformed so it becomes something else that is more valuable.

This process is mentioned in several places in Scripture, most notably in 2 Peter 1:3-4.

> His divine power has given us everything we need for a godly life through our knowledge of him who called us by his own glory and goodness. Through these he has given us his very great and precious promises, so that through them you may participate in the divine nature, having escaped the corruption in the world caused by evil desires.

Theosis even includes transformation of the body.

> But if Christ is in you, then even though your body is subject to death because of sin, the Spirit gives life because of righteousness. And if the Spirit of him who raised Jesus from the dead is living in you, he who raised Christ from the dead will also give life to your mortal bodies because of his Spirit who lives in you.[67]

The kundalini process plays a vital role in effecting this change as it opens energy passageways to allow God's Zoe to renew and re-order the energies of bios, psuche and pneuma. Spiritual re-birth and transformation entails a "re-wiring," of sorts, in all the levels of our being, and kundalini process is the means by which this happens. Of course, the body will eventually die, but while one continues to live, it will serve as

---

[67] Romans 8:10-11

the temple of the Holy Spirit.[68] One will live fully in Christ, and though outwardly we degenerate from the aging process, inwardly we are renewed daily by the Spirit of God.[69]

---

[68] 1 Cor. 6:19.

[69] 2 Cor. 4:16.

References

Listed below are books, articles and websites that are either cited in this work, or else are helpful resources for understanding kundalini in the spiritual life.

Arraj, James. *God, Zen and the Intuition of Being*. Chiloquin, OR: Inner Growth Books, 1988.

_____. *St. John of the Cross and Dr. C. G. Jung*. Chiloquin, OR: Inner Growth Books, *1986*.

Dixon, Jana. *Biology of Kundalini*. Raleigh, NC: Lulu Press, 2008.

Grof, Christina and Stanislov Grof. *The Stormy Search for the Self*. New York, NY: Jeremy P. Tarcher Ed., 1992.

Helminiak, Daniel. *Religion and the Human Sciences: An Approach via Spirituality*. Albany, NY: State University of New York Press, 1998.

Johnston, William. *Mystical Theology: The Science of Love*. New York, NY: HarperCollins, 1995.

Krishna, Gopi. *Kundalini: The Evolutionary Energy in Man*. Boston: Shambhala Publishing, 1985.

_____. *Kundalini for the New Age*. Gene Kieffer, ed. New York: Bantam Books, 1988.

_____. *Kundalini in Space and Time*. Institute for Consciousness Research. 2014.

Merton, Thomas. *Conjectures of a Guilty Bystander*. New York, NY: Image Books, 1968.

Myss, Carolyn. *Anatomy of the Spirit: The Seven Stages of Power and Healing*. New York, NY: Three Rivers Press, 1996.

Muktananda, Swami. *Kundalini: The Secret of Life*. South Fallsburg, NY: SYDA Foundation, 1979.

Pearce, Joseph Chilton. *From Magical Child to Magical Teen: A Guide to Adolescent Development*. Rochester, VT. Park Street Press, 2003.

Radha, Swami Sivananda. *Kundalini Yoga for the West*. Boston: Shambhala Publishing, 1985.

Royo, Antonio, O.P. and Jordan Aumann, O.P. *The Theology of Christian Perfection*. Dubuque, IA: Priory Press, 1962.

Sannella, Lee, M.D. *The Kundalini Experience*. Lower Lake, CA: Integral Publishing, 1987.

Siegal, Daniel. *Mind: A Journey to the Heart of Being Human*. New York, NY: W. W. Norton & Co., 2017.

St. John of the Cross. *Dark Night of the Soul*. (E. Allison Peers translation). Garden City, NY: Doubleday/Image., 1959.

St. Romain, Philip A. *Kundalini Energy and Christian Spirituality: A Pathway to Growth and Healing*. New York, NY: Crossroads Publ., 1991 1st edition. (2nd, revised edition by Lulu Press, 2010.)

_____. *God and I: Exploring the Connections Between God, Self and Ego*. Raleigh, NC: Lulu Press, 2016.

St. Thomas Aquinas. *The Summa Theologia*. New York, NY: Benziger Br., Inc. , 1947.

Streeter, Carla Mae. *Foundations of Spirituality: A Systematic Approach*. Collegeville, MN: Michael Glazier, 2012.

U. S. Catholic Church. *The Catechism of the Catholic Church*. U. S. Catholic Conference. 1994.

U. S. Conference of Catholic Bishops. Guidelines for Evaluating Reiki as an Alternative Therapy. http://www.usccb.org/_cs_upload/8092_1.pdf 2009.

Washburn, Michael. *The Ego and the Dynamic Ground: A Transpersonal Theory of Human Development.* Albany, NY: State University of New York Press, 1988.

_____. *Embodied Spirituality is a Sacred World*, p. 221. (Albany, NY: State University of New York Press, 2003)

Yun, Koo Dong. *The Holy Spirit and Ch'i (Qi): A Chiological Approach to Pneumatology.* Eugene, OR: Wipf and Stock Publ., 2012

Appendix 1
Kundalini and the Holy Spirit

A few points originally published on the kundalini discussion forum, August 8, 2001.

1. There are two "directions" that interplay in the spiritual life.
a. the human reaching for God.
b. God reaching for the human.

2. It seems to me that some Eastern spiritualities build upon the dynamism of the human reaching for God, while the Judeo-Christian-Islam traditions emphasize God reaching for the human. These are generalizations, of course, but I think they have merit.

3. The kundalini experience of an energy latent in most people, which becomes awakened/ignited, opens the metaphysical energy centers (chakras), and culminates with union with God in the 7th center is a superb expression of the Eastern dynamism. The kundalini process is an "ascent" from almost sub-human levels of concern and intelligence to "super-human" levels. As such, it has been called an "evolutionary energy" by Gopi Krishna and others, who view kundalini as the key to awakening and developing the fullness of our human potential and awakening us to a sense of cosmic consciousness and union with God and creation.

4. The Christian description of the Holy Spirit is of a "descent" from above mediated by Christ, Who gives the Spirit to transform a person unto his own Blessed consciousness. As one of the Persons of the Trinity, this Spirit

is also present in all of creation, flowing through the Word and returning to the Father, and so it is present in all the world religions and responsible for the fruits of the Spirit wherever they are manifest. Flowing through Christ, the Incarnation of the Word, the Spirit works to build a new humanity in the likeness of Christ.

5. The intermingling of the human evolutionary spirit of ascent (kundalini) and the descending Spirit of blessing (Holy Spirit) are sure to happen in Christians who are eager for growth in the Spirit. We shouldn't be surprised to find an ignition/activation of the kundalini dynamism in Christians who generously open themselves to grow in the Spirit through charismatic prayer, centering prayer, and other prayer forms that invite the Spirit to work.

6. It is possible at times to be in touch with the kundalini dynamism without sensing much of the Spirit. The converse is also true. Obviously, both are often experienced together, and can be mutually complementary. But in my experience, at least, there is a difference between the two that is possible to discern.

7. The gift of the Spirit might be viewed, then, as a means by which the kundalini process is awakened in some Christians, and the Intelligence by means of which the kundalini dynamism is integrated so that the Christian grows into the fullness of his/her evolutionary destiny in Christ. This can be experienced in the life of individuals, to some extent, but moreso in the human family through time.

8. Therefore, it is easy to see how Christians who experience kundalini process during the course of their growth in the Spirit can often conclude that kundalini and the Spirit are one and the same.

9. However, one must note as well that there are many who evidence kundalini awakening without manifesting the fruits of the Spirit, and others who manifest the fruits of the Spirit without kundalini awakening.

10. Christians have much to learn from the yogic traditions on kundalini in Hinduism concerning how this energy works and how to integrate it. Care must be taken, however, to avoid viewing the differences in teachings on the Spirit and kundalini as merely semantical. One key criterion is to ask whether those the other tradition would agree with one's assessment: e.g., would a Hindu agree that the way Christians describe the Spirit is the same as their understanding of kundalini? would Christians (the Church) agree that the ascent of Shakti through the chakras and central channel to union with Shiva above the head is a good way to understand the working of the Spirit in a Christian's life? Clearly, more dialogue between these traditions is needed before these questions can be answered.

Appendix 2
Kundalini Stories

Most of the stories below were shared with me via email or on my kundalini discussion board. Permission was obtained to use them, though I am publishing them all pseudonymously. Additionally, a few stories were published on the innerexplorations.com web site, with permission to reprint them obtained from Tyra Arraj. I have changed nothing in the accounts below except for a few cases of misspelled words. Terminology is sometimes at odds with the approach taken in this book, but has not been changed.

Approximately 20 years ago, around 1995, I was invited to attend a "meditation workshop" by a dear friend. It was given by the Sahaja Yoga community.

I attended and a simple meditation was performed. What happened to me was unexpected and intense! I left that workshop that evening with an enormous burst of flowing energy from my crown chakra that was incredibly strong and lasted for a month! The intensity began to dissipate but I still feel it today off and on, especially during spiritual occasions.

On the night this occurred I went home to my husband and told him what had happened. He told me that it appeared my kundalini had risen. He told me some people work all their lives for this to happen and he was amazed that it occurred to me! The next week my husband and a few of our friends decided to attend the same session! Nothing could keep them away! I can say, however, that of our friends, only my husband had a similar experience to the one I had. It was amazing and remains amazing now, twenty years later!

- by Anon1

I have always wanted to be "real" since I can remember. I used to celebrate mass in my bedroom when I was a small child, inviting the local kids to receive ice cream wafers from my hands.

I began practicing meditation when I was in my early thirties. I am now 69. I think that the first noticeable kundalini episode occurred for me while I was on a silent retreat in the 1980s. During the celebration of Mass I was waiting to receive a Communion host from a minister of the Eucharist when I suddenly began to shake and burn up from my toes to my head. I tried to stand still, and the woman seemed to notice and immediately said, "May this bring you healing." This was the beginning of several kundalini episodes and am still experiencing kundalini syndrome 25 years later. All I desired was union with God; nothing else mattered. I used to read the Christian mystics' experience of God/ Other over and over again. I was filled with desire for God but not fully realizing that this was to be a profound and powerful physical, psychological and spiritual experience that would turn my world upside down. My spiritual director created a safe space for my ramblings of a mystical nature, although most of the time she hadn't a clue about my strange ramblings of my spiritual experiences.

Meditation was my daily practice with occasionally experiencing total bliss. Once while sitting alone in my local church I "disappeared" into a huge ball of golden light becoming aware of the core of who I was. I had found my truth. This experience of pure light caused me to write over and over again my magnificat. I lost track of time in this blissful state but I spent the following weeks in tears of joy as I sensed such union with everything. I don't know how long this went on for, but the ecstatic feelings finally settled down eventually with just the assurance that no matter what happens in this life that all is well. All is well. I felt that all fear was gone. This was the first of three kundalini episodes each of which were profoundly physical and triggered by the combination of deep prayer; once by acupuncture needle to the crown of my skull which opened me up to my repressed feelings and memories, and a year long bedridden "virus," and the most recent which was major surgery which opened up my psyche to more and more unconscious material. I would not have gone through these powerful physical and spiritual transformational processes had I not had the gifted presence of my spiritual director and body oriented therapist, both who kept me grounded and safe.

My journey has been a physically and emotionally painful one, entailing months in bed, releasing powerful feelings and energetic jerks and primal sounds, but with each episode I grew more and more compassionate, loving, and most of all more real. I learned to surrender over and over again. I now know what Adyashanti means when he says that awakening is "absolute cooperation with the inevitable." And at the same time there are times when I remind "God," in the words of St Teresa of Avila, "If this is how you treat your friends, its no wonder you have so few!!" and yet I wouldn't change it for the world.

- by Anon2

My kundalini experience emerged from a change in how I relate to my brain. I had just been accepted into a Masters program, although I struggled with adult ADD and had an awful time focusing my attention when attempting to read. While looking for ways to help myself in this dilemma I stumbled upon binaural recordings, specifically a low beta recording designed to increase focus. I immediately found myself able to keep my mind stayed on the words in front of me without drifting off to other thoughts. Prior to this experience I was so identified as my mind that never considered that it was an instrument that I held the power to direct. This led me to explore other recordings that could enhance my life experience. I came across one called "Awakening the Kundalini" by Kelly Howell and dove right in. Little did I know that the outcome was about to change the entire course of my life. I did the meditation and breathing exercises and found myself caught up in an expansive sense of orgasmic pleasure and oneness with all that is. My world broke open to an inner expanse I had only tasted in the past through much prayer and silence.

This experience did not simply fade away but the next year was filled with a sense of awe, bliss and at times terror as the source energies collided with the fears of my rigid religious background. I had spent most of my adult life as a devoted Evangelical/Pentecostal. I had been a street preacher, intercessor and missionary to Central Asian Muslims. This experience was the exact thing I had warned others about. I had considered it to be a satanic deception and I was now immersed in its power. I felt this energy in my groin almost continually for the first year as if a small electric motor had been implanted there. I would often awaken in the morning with a sense of bliss, as if I was seeing the beauty around me for the first time. At other times I would be gripped by an existential fear of damnation from my religious training and what I now know, was my ego's terror of being found a fraud. The genuineness of the bliss and the taste of liberation drove me to cooperate with this energy rather than fight it.

This cooperation eventually led to a more stable relationship with this divine energy in my life. I studied the roots of my experience in Hinduism and mystical traditions from all religions and was particularly drawn to Advaita/Vedanta. I have explored many practices that enhanced my life and let them go when it was time to move on. These have included traditional chakra mediation, ecstatic dance, sacred sound mediations and tantric practices focused on the divine feminine. I will be forever grateful for this divine power that put me on the path of self-inquiry.

- by Anon3

When I was a young man about 20 years old I was deeply committed to intercessory prayer, there was a convenient chapel a walking distance from my apartment that was open 24/7. I would go down into the chapel and pray crying out to heaven, praying for hours on end. Sensing burdens and often feeling my mouth go numb from the praying out loud for hours on end there were several times I was so lost in prayer that when I emerged from the chapel it was the following morning and I had prayed through the night. This went on for several days a week, week after week for several months. I then began to experience some amazing physical sensations up and down my spine as if a hot molten fire was pushing itself up my spine. Sometimes it would be like hot electrical sparks these were accompanied by visions and enormous empathic ability to feel the emotions and inner conditions of others hearts. The experiences got so profound that I had to retreat to a place away from people and I would weep before the Lord and find myself in surrendered worship for 6 to

8 hours a day. I was unable to eat food for 22 days; it was not like a fast; there was simply no desire for food to enter my body — no hunger pains. Unfortunately, I had no teaching available to explain what was happening and there were times I thought I was simply just losing my mind as my body would shake and quiver with rushes of ecstatic energy and bliss, the world became so alive so full of color and sensory meaning, that when the experience finally receded I experienced a type of depression at the blandness the world had returned to so far from its true expression. It was years later I learned in Jewish mystical traditions that the holy spark of God consciousness embedded in our sacrum could be liberated back up to God up the spine.

- by Anon4

Devoted Christian until about the age of 18 when began to wander into drug culture (And here's something interesting - kundalini and drug use). 7 years ago, aged 24, began experiencing these symptoms - burning sensation at the base of my spine, hearing my name called as I lay to sleep, sensation of a bird flying around inside me, energy rushes - sometimes blissful; other times anxious, burning in my body, telepathic sensitivity, precognition. Because I was unprepared and on drugs I had a weird mental breakdown. Every night, when I went to bed, conversations and scenarios filled my head. I thought I had tapped into some collective consciousness.

Eventually gave up drugs and things settled down. My research into what had happened to me led me to a knowledge of Kundalini and Eastern mysticism - so I explored. Got involved with new age groups, spiritual healers, practiced yoga and all kinds of taoist exercises.

Then I began to suffer psychic attacks and for a while 3 years ago went thru a traumatic time. These attacks sprang from fool-hardy practice and association with "healers" and I found that I was living in a massive deja vu. Everything I had heard as voices while lying in bed at night during my mental breakdown was now being lived thru, 3 years on. I felt trapped, was completely traumatized.

I have recovered and given myself to Christ once again, although I still suffer attacks from dangerous individuals, not demons but occultists. Indeed just this month psychic channels have re-opened after contact with a Christian healer. I am very attracted by Charismatic worship and praise and go to a local charismatic church but find that there is a confusion with the work of the Holy Spirit and kundalini in what they do and that there is an ignorance of the relationship between Charismatic phenomena and kundalini.

- by Anon5

I am a thirty year old female, and I experienced kundalini about three and a half years ago. At first, I had some energy problems - I really didn't know what I was doing or what I was getting into - but these days, all this seems to have settled down. I am these days a practicing Christian, having converted after my kundalini experience (which occurred during Easter). I think that in many ways, it has helped me to cope with it. Maybe it is not for me to judge, but over the past few years, I feel that I have met many people who were just "nominal" Christians. However, I also feel that I've met a few who were sincere in their faith, and who were truly "anointed." I accept that not all people are drawn to the mystical side of things, and nowadays think that perhaps it not always necessary to have been through a powerful kind of experience like kundalini in order to have a strong relationship with God. I have read many stories about people who have experienced kundalini and suffered some very harmful effects. To me, yes it is preferable to have had a stable grounding built up over many years through dedicated prayer and study, rather than put oneself through this. Kundalini is something I'd really only recommend to people who are very mature, stable and responsible - not to young and impressionable people who are mainly out for the thrill of an "out of this world" type experience, because having had the experience, you then have to deal with it and the repercussions over the long term, for the rest of your life. Whichever way you choose, to me what is most important is the way in which you transmit your faith/beliefs/experiences to your overall life. I wish to thank you for providing an open, balanced discussion and forum on this often very heated topic.

- Anon6

A brief history. I grew up in a Christian environment, and throughout my life, I never questioned that God existed. But I also didn't ever have a connection there. I believed because I couldn't fathom how everything could exist so perfectly otherwise, but my prayers were mostly just "talking out loud in case someone was listening."

I landed in a Kundalini Yoga studio in July. I had no knowledge of kundalini and was basically looking for an exercise program. However, in that first class, I immediately felt like I was in the right place. Something just resonated intensely with me, and I went to 21 classes my first month. I'd never committed to anything like that ever! The mantras, the pranayama...it was all so lovely and just fit for some reason. The timing was most perfect, too. I'd been off alcohol for a year (high function/high bottom), but I was struggling with an emotional low. In yoga, I felt something. Something wonderful.

It wasn't until a couple of months in that I really started reading about kundalini. Around September or October during one of the meditations, I had the sensation that my head was open with a roaring waterfall of light pouring in. It startled me! Since then I continue to have:

- sensations of light shining on my head
- burning that rotates among my heart, solar plexus and navel centers (my heart is on fire now)
- feelings of a sunlamp type of heat on my head (forehead/top) or on my back
- hot spine in class
- 4 a.m. wake ups (I was always a very sound sleeper)
- occasional night sweats
- flashes of light when I close my eyes at night or a single purple beam of light moving around my head/face
- awakening to realize I am buzzing or vibrating
- sleep paralysis, or waking up with the inability to move
- a beautiful glow of soft, warming light enveloping me in meditation

I have read one shouldn't pursue kundalini. Well, I guess I did, but it wasn't planned that way. But now here I am (right??), although pre-full blown awakening. I'm scared by some of what I read. I'm nervous to move forward, but I'm also afraid of going backward. From what I understand, I don't know that I could get off this ride now even if I wanted to...? I guess that's why I'm posting and what my question is. Even if it weren't too late, I would have a hard time quitting. The connected feeling is just so....divine.

- Anon7

I learned the Jesus prayer back in 1978. Over the years I have practiced the Prayer of the Heart or the Jesus Prayer both as a passive meditation and as an active meditation. It has just become a normal way of life and part of my consciousness. There have been times when I was upset and automatically the Jesus Prayer starts up and I am praying it or I am praying in tongues quietly. If I am upset or nervous or anxious about something the Jesus Prayer helps to quiet me down and brings peace.

There have been times when I was sleeping and had a nightmare and the Jesus Prayer started within me in the dream and I would wake up. When this happens I imagine myself saying the prayer and hear it within, then it wakes me up. If there is an accident or something happens suddenly the name of Jesus rises up within me often. . .

Oftentimes the Jesus Prayer becomes praying in tongues or tongues leads into praise which becomes the Jesus Prayer. The gift of tongues and the Jesus Prayer are about equal in importance in my inner life. But there is something special about the gift of tongues that is supernatural and deeper than most meditations. . .

There have been times of meditation when I seemed to be going deep inside and heading towards joy and peace but then, then anger or lust or other vice enters in and it is as if I start sinking down or spiraling down into darkness and gloom. As this spiraling down continues the negative emotions, vices, becomes the main focus and my consciousness moves to the meditation and I need to start the invocation "Jesus Christ son of God have mercy on me a sinner." One of the 'mercy' invocations like 'Jesus have mercy on me', is the best invocation to use during these times of darkness and negative emotions. The Jesus prayer reverses the downward spiral and moves my being, my consciousness spiraling upwards.

Doing stretching, yoga or Pilates are helpful in preparing for passive meditation and to channel the energy giving peace. This led me into creating the Rosary Postures (Rosary Yoga, a posture for every rosary bead prayer) which has been very helpful in developing my meditation.

There are times of meditation when I go deeply into it as if to a center point in my being and then experienced a rising of energy up my spine, as if an energy force is shooting up my spine. This is often referred to as kundalini. This can be very powerful and even bring on a little shaking or raising up of ones hands. Oftentimes when this happens I would go from a quiet still point within myself to raising my arms and entering into charismatic praise. Usually the rising of the energy in my spinal column is accompanied by a joy or experience of momentary bliss. It's as if there's an expansion of my consciousness accompanied by a pervasive light, glowing within.

This experience is very similar to charismatic praise in which there is a point of intensity in the praise that my arms automatically raised up. When this happens there is often a rush up my spine which lifts my hands up as I praise God! This is a common experience among charismatics, especially at prayer meetings.

  - Anon8

I am a new kundalini Christian. I think I am about 11 or so years into transformation. I am currently at the point of body vibrations mainly felt when I wake up at night and for the last year K Awakening seems to be focused on my head/brain I believe. Before the body vibrations started I felt a pressure in my head, mainly at the sixth chakra. I let it do its thing over a few days and my body felt like it was being scanned from my eye brows down to the tips of my toes literally. I think it was looking for any problem areas. A few times after that it felt like energy rush up and out of me. I think it was testing my system and making a connection. My newest symptom if you will is tenderness on the crown and back of my head. I have the usual bugs crawling, itching, ears constantly ringing and static kind of feeling but that feels like the normal everyday occurrences you just get used to. Is it possible to timeline how much further we have to go......months, years? The main reason I am reaching out is to see if anyone can give me any kind of advice.....pre- and pos-t full-blown K awakening? What to do? What not to do? What to watch out for, what to run with? An example question is when I begin to see and hear in the spirit, is there anything to watch for in regards to discernment? I know that everything that sparkles isn't good. Is there literature to read to prepare? Is a specific type of meditation recommended or should that be avoided?

- Anon9

The first time I had a kundalini experience (at age 50) was near the end of a month-long yoga teacher training at the Kripalu Yoga Center in Lennox, MA. I had a strong connection with one of our teacher trainers, a woman who had also just turned 50. At the end of a class, in lieu of savasana, she cued the refinements of Mountain Pose. I followed along with all the alignment checks from the ground up—feet in firm contact with the earth, knees soft, etc. At last, when I reached up through my crown, I felt a bolt of white light surge up through the ground and out the top of my head. It was a very brief experience, neither painful nor pleasurable, however I consider it the "Road to Damascus Moment" in my personal journey. Neither my training as a psychologist, nor my early religious training as a Catholic provided any point of reference for understanding what had just happened—nothing in my previous experience or circumstances did. It was as though I had been dope-slapped by the Universe: *What you know or think you know, Sister, isn't much.*

For months, I didn't tell anyone much about it, with the exception of my husband Jonathan, who is supremely supportive of me (and, as a scientist, curious about all natural phenomena). After returning home from Kripalu, I had other energy experiences. One that stands out in my mind happened while I was doing yoga nidra. I had propped myself in savasana with a blanket, bolster, etc., and I started having painful abdominal cramps. I knew I'd feel fine if I did wind-relieving pose, but then…I would have to rearrange my props…and I was so deep into meditation. After a few minutes the cramps became unbearable, so finally I hugged my knee to my chest, the pipes gurgled, and I felt much better. When I opened my eyes to re-prop myself, there was not so much as a wrinkle in the blanket that needed straightening out. The sensations I had experienced were identical to those I have in the physical practice of yoga, but I had moved only in my energy body. I told one of my teacher trainers about the experience, a yogi with thirty years of practice, and all he had to say was, "Wow." I felt unnerved.

Why were things happening to me that seemed so out-of-the-ordinary, even to a seasoned yogi?

In the seven years since then, I have had numerous other energy experiences, weeks or months apart. Other than the first kundalini experience I had, the only other one that had a profound effect on my outlook happened last summer while on another four-day retreat at Kripalu. It was a CEU training for Internal Family Systems therapy, mostly focused on work with trauma survivors. One of the training videos featured a client who was a social worker with bipolar disorder, who had been sexually abused as a toddler, and who felt victimized by episodes of mania—all problems I have personally experienced. The next morning I did a leisurely yoga practice with a lot of hip and pelvic floor stretches. When I was resting in savasana afterward, waves of blissful energy pulsed up my legs and into my pelvis for a few minutes. I vividly experienced being healed and whole, especially in my svadisthana chakra, genitals, and pelvis. I was in a floating bliss for the rest of the day. I ate an enormous heavy meal that night (including a glass of wine and two loaves of Italian bread I just about saturated with olive oil) which helped bring my energies down to a level I found more comfortable and familiar. For the next two weeks I felt a profound love for everyone and everything—life just seemed sweet through and through. Gradually these feelings began to dissipate, and for another couple of weeks I was hyper-aware of the impermanence of all things, brooding on topics such as the mortality of my step-children, whom I adore. I didn't experience the usual symptoms I associate with depression, such as irritability, self-loathing, etc. I felt awed and sobered at the impermanence of all things in the universe. Writing about these kundalini experiences feels a little abstract now. I wonder where they went and how to live my life in light of them. If I had not studied non-dualism (with Richard Miller, a yoga nidra teacher in the Advaita Vedanta tradition who was a student of Jean Klein), I am sure I would have taken the extremes of my experience last summer at face value, rather than as messengers, and that the effect on my mental health would have been disastrous.

- Anon10

My first experience with the energy known as kundalini was at 30 years old as I participated in a 10 day intensive centering prayer retreat hosted by Contemplative Outreach at a Trappist monastery. There, I developed a constant pain in the center of my chest. It came on suddenly and wouldn't leave, a pressure sensation that was uncomfortable. I spoke to Father Keating, the retreat leader, about this but he did not venture any guesses as to what it could be. I had heard of kundalini and the chakra system but knew very little. I made the connection between kundalini and my pain but was disappointed and anxious as there was no mention of this type of experience by Father Keating although he mentioned a book by Mr. St. Romain. I could find no Catholic reference to the subject of energy centers and relied on books of yogis such as Gopi Krishna and Shyam Sundar Goswami. To my great relief I read Philip St. Romain's book on Christianity and kundalini. It was the only link I had to my faith and energy systems.

From *Open Mind, Open Heart* by Father Thomas Keating I learned about the unloading of the unconscious emotional junk that happens with centering prayer practice. From Gopi Krishna I learned about the negative affects of kundalini if it encountered a system that is impure, i.e. anxiety, fear, tension, depression, cravings, etc. The pain in my center chest eased gradually over time. With daily centering prayer I enjoyed about 3 years of bliss and ecstasies, great love of God and peace. Then came the opposite. I was overwhelmed. I had many unresolved life issues and bad habits that also negatively effected the process of unloading and life energy movement. I spent the next 15 years with intense insecurity, social phobia, shame, fear, body dismorphic disorder, anxiety, difficulty concentrating, flushing, and boundary issues. I owe so much to a number of helpful books and to a therapist with whom I had rapport and who helped me heal. Also, an important dream shone light on the origin of much of my shame.

The social fallout of this 15 year period was the inability to go to Mass due to social phobia, alienation at work, and fear of rejection. I removed myself from an unhealthy peer group to help heal. There were physical manifestations of kundalini. I began to see bright blue dots during periods of interested attention to an idea, and then violet areas during yoga stretches and centering prayer. Pressure in my forehead and down my nose, an irritation tickle in my throat, and pressure on the top of my head were also common. There were times of sexual intensity and the base of my spine feeling cold. There was a flash of white light a few times, hot and sweaty hands, and a sparkly energy in the top of my head. There were "hot spots" inside my head, cool liquid feelings deep in the ear and later coming up the sides of my neck. There was for years pain at the stigmata points of my hands and feet, and I felt like I had a painful broken heart. I had 4 root canals in 1 1/2 years. My face scrunched up during centering. I learned that I needed to take care of my body by exercising, eating healthy, doing yoga stretches and sleeping 9 hours a night.

Spiritually I was seeking, praying, and reading. I compared and contrasted religions. I let go of rigidity and fell in love with the face of Jesus.

7 years later.

In a surprising occurrence of synchronicity, I was handed a shed snakeskin on 1-1-15. In January in Minnesota it is not usual to see snake skins and it proved to be the beginning of a period of new life for me. I had just received a book on St. Hildegard of Bingen. I was hooked. In her I found the bringing together of my love of God and nature. She gave me a way forward. I planted a garden with vegetables and medicinal plants. I got bee hives and soon plan to raise chickens. Maybe goats. She brought me back to the Church and I have a love of the Mass, confession and adoration I never knew before. I am still centering, praying lectio divina and my love of the Holy Face of Jesus grows continually. I have a spiritual director and a new love of our Mother Mary. I wear an Immaculate Conception medal. I am working 45 hours a week. Our family has grown from 2 children to 2 married children and 5 grandchildren (with one on the way). The work I did with cognitive therapy has been effective in relieving anxiety and shame. I still love solitude and am still rather private and cautious in social situations. I keep my boundaries and flushing has turned to hot flashes. My ecstasies flow instead of stopping me. I still have occasional trouble with intense emotions. The hot and cool sensations come and go. I still see colors. The terrible heartache is gone with the help of St. Hildegard's remedies. Her dietary recommendations have promoted a healthy digestive system with no more intestinal cramps. Mostly, I live an intentional life in the hope of the Lord. God bless.

- Anon11

About six months before I noticed kundalini awakening symptoms, I was looking for ways to become more involved at my church. At that time, a small group was offering a series of lectures on the Catholic Charismatic Renewal. There were many aspects of the spirituality that did not resonate with me, but I regularly attended the group meetings, keeping in mind that it wasn't about what I wanted but rather what God may want to show me through this experience. Thus, we prayed for each other for baptism in the Holy Spirit, for the various charisms, for forgiveness and purification, and for healing. Together we went for healing masses, charismatic conferences and other similar events.

During those gatherings, I began experiencing various subtle phenomena, both spiritual and energetic. At one healing Mass, I felt an emanation of God's immense tenderness coming from the speaker as he blessed me, and from the crucifix he held over my head streamed a beam of heat. I could also also feel a magnetic field around my hands when I prayed, and on occasion, an inner vibration in my arms or a flutter rising up my torso. My energy levels increased and my need for sleep became less. At the charismatic healing conference, I remember feeling disappointed that I would not have the opportunity to be called up for prayer for a migraine that had come on earlier that morning. At that very moment, the charismatic evangelist stopped in mid sentence and said, "There is someone here with a headache...." I believe that that conference was the tipping point, for those four days were teaming with the magnificent work of the Holy Spirit and I was unable to sleep because my entire body vibrated so intensely.

Not long after that event, I came down with intolerable back pain that refused to respond to any intervention. Once I connected it to some painful childhood experiences, I cried half the pain out. The other half, I took the lead from the examples at the healing conference, and cast it out in the name of Jesus. The pain left instantly. Two weeks of unprovoked tears followed. As soon as the water hit my body during my morning shower, I would begin to sob without knowing exactly why. My morning prayers were equally tearful and they were easily two hours long even though they felt like ten minutes. During this period, I began to experience visual symptoms, the expanding, billowing lights of various colors. In the next phase, I was overwhelmed with a euphoric yearning for God and a desire to go to Mass.

Since then I have experienced nearly every kundalini awakening symptom on the list. The most prominent have been the nightly leg/body jerks, pressure at the third eye and a mild, pleasant vibration throughout my body, all which vary from time to time in intensity. The psycho-spirtual phenomena have included vivd, lucid dreaming, visions, bursts of light during prayer, and physical and emotional healing. I would characterize the process thus far as a bit wild and perplexing, but generally not negative. It has made my spiritual journey infinitely richer. I feel deep inner calm which allows me to navigate through the world better.

- Anon12

About the Author

Philip St. Romain, M.S., D. Min., is the author of numerous books on Christian spirituality and theology, including *Jesus Alive in Our Lives, Kundalini Energy and Christian Spirituality: A Pathway to Growth and Healing,* and *Praying the Daily Gospels.* For the past 30 years, he has worked in retreat ministry as a spiritual director and retreat master. Currently, he works with Heartland Center for Spirituality in Great Bend, KS. He is married with three grown children, residing in Bel Aire, KS, which is just outside of Wichita.

See www.philstromain.com for more information.